PS8565.U54 B43

Hunter, Maureen

Beautiful Lake

1990, c198

5

16.2

MW01122014

2002 03 05

HUMBER COLLEGE L. R. C. (LAKESHORE)

Beautiful Lake Winnipeg first published 1990 by
Blizzard Publishing Ltd.
301–89 Princess St., Winnipeg, Canada R3B 1K6
© 1989 Maureen Hunter

Cover design by Terry Gallagher
Cover photo by Jo-Anne Ford
Author photo by Jean Hunter
Printed in Canada by Hignell Printing Ltd.

Printed with the assistance of the Manitoba Arts Council.

Caution

This play is fully protected under the copyright laws of Canada and
all other countries of the Copyright Union and is subject to royalty.
Rights to produce, in whole or part, by any group amateur or
professional, are retained by the author.

No part of this book (including cover design) may be reproduced
or transmitted in any form, by any means, electronic or mechanical,
including photocopying, recording, and information storage and
retrieval systems, without permission in writing from the publisher,
except by a reviewer, who may quote brief passages in a review.

Canadian Cataloguing in Publication Data
    Hunter, Maureen, 1947–
        Beautiful Lake Winnipeg
        A play
        ISBN 0–921368–10–0
    I. Title.
    PS8565.U5814B4 1990   C812'.54   C90–097012–X
    PR9199.3.H858B4

160201

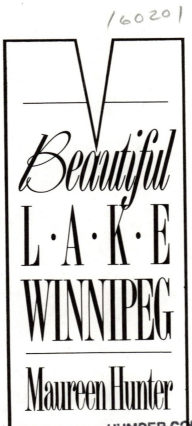

Beautiful L·A·K·E WINNIPEG

Maureen Hunter

HUMBER COLLEGE
LAKESHORE CAMPUS
LEARNING RESOURCE CENTRE
3199 LAKESHORE BLVD. WEST
TORONTO, ONTARIO M8V 1K8

Blizzard Publishing • Winnipeg

LAKESHORE CAMPUS
LEARNING RESOURCE CENTRE
3199 LAKESHORE BLVD WEST

BEAUTIFUL LAKE WINNIPEG was first produced at
the Manitoba Theatre Centre's Warehouse Theatre in
Winnipeg on January 24, 1990, with the following cast:

MITCH	Robert Bockstael
SALOME	Rosalie Rudelier
IAN	David Storch
ALIDA	Patricia Vanstone

Directed by Larry Desrochers
Set and Costumes Designed by Carole Klemm
Lighting Designed by Hugh Connacher
Original Music Composed by Randolph Peters
Stage Managed by Dianne Domaratzki

The playwright is grateful to the following for their
contribution to the development of this play: the
Manitoba Arts Council; Manitoba Association of
Playwrights; Manitoba Theatre Centre; the members of
the 1986–87 Playwrights Unit (PTE/MAP); Playwrights
Workshop Montreal (Svetlana Zylin); Larry Desrochers;
Gary Hunter; Stephanie Kostiuk; George Toles.

The publishers would like to thank Maureen Devanik
for all her help.

For Gary

CHARACTERS

IAN: Alida's fiancé.
MITCH: Alida's ex-husband.
ALIDA: Owner of the cottage.
SALOME: A woman of the lake.
(Salome is pronounced "Sal-o-may")

SCENE

A clearing outside a cottage on a remote shore of Lake Winnipeg. Early September.

The cottage is small, old and quite run-down. It sits at an angle, running from down left to up center. A railed-in porch runs across the front; three wide steps lead up to it. Under the porch is a crawl space; part of it is enclosed with decrepit lattice-work and part of it is open and used for storage (lawn chairs, lanterns, etc.). A wooden door, locked and padlocked, leads off the porch into the cottage. Next to the door is a multi-paned, casement style window, locked from inside. One of the panes is broken.

In the clearing around the cottage are trees and shrubs, all natural to the area. The only piece of furniture is a weathered, wooden picnic table, which stands near the steps.

There are three entrances. One (off right) leads to the lake; the other two run on either side of the cottage, one leading to the cars and to Salome's, the other leading to the barbecue. The entrances are partly screened by shrubs.

Act One

Scene One

(Friday, 7:30 p.m. IAN enters. He's under 30, with clean-cut good looks and an athletic build. He wears fashionable summer clothes. He is loaded down with supplies: a cooler, bags of groceries, overnight bags, etc. Dangling from his teeth is a set of car keys. He almost loses part of his load on entering, steadies himself, moves next to the steps and more or less lets things fall. Then he pockets the keys, glances around the clearing, moves down right and stares off.)

IAN: *(Displeased.)* Great. Terrific.

(He turns back upstage, studies the cottage from a distance. He moves to the table, tests it for strength, does the same with the porch railing—more out of boredom than interest. He climbs the steps to the cottage, tries the door and the window; both are locked. He peers through the window into the dark interior of the cottage. Then he leaves the porch, discovers the open crawl space underneath and hauls out a couple of decrepit collapsible chairs. He leans them against the porch. Next he pulls out a lantern and a tin box containing candles and matches, which he spills. He stifles a

*curse, gathers up the candles and matches and sets
them on the table. He rummages through the stuff
he carried on and sets out a bottle of liquor, a roll
of plastic glasses and a six-pack of beer. He opens
a beer, shoves the rest into the cooler. He moves
back down right and stares off. A beat. He turns
back up-stage. Another beat.)*

What the hell am I supposed to do now?

*(He moves back to the porch, picks up a lounge-
type chair, carries it down right and sets it up. He
sits, but the angle of the back is wrong. He stifles
another curse. He gets up, adjusts the chair, sits
again. A beat.)*

Terrific. No music, no books. Nothing.

*(He sits staring gloomily off as MITCH enters,
tossing a set of keys. He's a dark, powerfully-built
man, about 40, wearing a casual shirt, jeans,
runners. IAN turns toward him, waits for him to
speak. He doesn't.)*

Looking for someone?

MITCH: Yeah.

IAN: Who?

MITCH: Alida.

IAN: She's not here right now.

MITCH: Where is she?

IAN: *(Stands, moves toward him.)* Maybe I can help you.
I'm not too familiar with the place, but—

MITCH: Where is she!

IAN: *(Stops moving.)* She's out.

MITCH: Out, fuck. 'Til when?

IAN: Look, uh … how would you like to tell me who you are?

MITCH: How would you like to tell *me* who you are.

IAN: Ian Holden. I'm her fiancé.

MITCH: Her what?

IAN: Her fiancé.

MITCH: *(Grins.)* Her fiancé! No shit.

IAN: And you are—?

MITCH: Mitch, the name's Mitch. *(Enjoys it.)* I'm her husband.

(An awkward moment for IAN.)

IAN: Well! I'm … *(Moves to him, offers his hand.)* Pleased to meet you.

MITCH: Are you?

(A beat. IAN withdraws his hand.)

IAN: What, uh … what are you doing here?

MITCH: I could ask you the same question.

IAN: Not really.

MITCH: I just did.

IAN: I'm here with Alida. That should be obvious.

MITCH: Should it?

IAN: I think so.

MITCH: Then where is she?

IAN: I told you, she's out.

MITCH: Out where?

IAN: Look, man I—

MITCH: *(Like a shotgun blast.)* Mitch!

IAN: Sorry?

MITCH: The name is Mitch, didn't I just tell you? Don't call me man. Ever!

IAN: *(Beat.)* Mitch.

MITCH: You got it.

    (MITCH saunters down center.)

IAN: I think you should explain why you're here.

MITCH: You do, eh.

IAN: Definitely.

MITCH: All right, I'll explain. I'm here to see Alida.

IAN: Why?

MITCH: We've got a little business to clear up.

IAN: Business.

MITCH: Yeah, business. How long's she going to be, anyway?

IAN: I don't know.

MITCH: You don't know?

IAN: I don't know. Sorry.

MITCH: Fine. I'll wait.

    (He picks up a chair.)

IAN: Here?

MITCH: Where else?

IAN: Well, there's a motel down the highway. A café about a mile back.

MITCH: I know that, fuck, you going to draw me a map?

(He carries the chair down center.)

IAN: Aw, look, man—

MITCH: *(An explosion.)* Mitch!

IAN: Right, I—

MITCH: Don't make me say it again!

IAN: *(Takes a breath.)* What I was going to suggest—
Mitch—is that if you go back to that motel, and wait
there, I'll have her call you as soon as she gets back.

MITCH: You will, huh.

IAN: You have my word on it.

MITCH: Yeah? Well, your word's worth shit. There's no
phone here.

IAN: No phone?

MITCH: No phone.

IAN: Well then, I'll drive her over. You go back to that
motel, have yourself a cup of coffee, and I'll drive her
over the minute she gets back. All right?

　　(MITCH snaps the chair open.)

I'm asking you to wait somewhere else. No offence.

MITCH: I heard you. *(Sits.)* No offence.

　　(A beat. IAN laughs uncomfortably.)

IAN: You're serious. You really want to do this.

MITCH: Why not?

IAN: It's a bit awkward, wouldn't you say?

MITCH: No.

IAN: No. Well, it's awkward as hell for me.

MITCH: Well then, maybe you should leave.

IAN: I'm here with Alida!

MITCH: Are you? I don't know that, do I?

IAN: What's that supposed to mean?

MITCH: Well, where is she?

IAN: She's out.

MITCH: So you keep telling me but what I'm saying is, how do I know for sure? Maybe you made it up. Maybe you don't even know my wife, maybe you're just some intruder who's set up camp here. I mean, the door's locked, isn't it? How come the door's locked, if you're here with Alida?

IAN: This is crazy, you know that? I mean, I don't know whether to laugh, or ... *(Trails off, takes a breath.)* You want to know why the door's locked. It's locked because she left in a hurry, and she took the key with her. Okay? She just—she forgot.

MITCH: She must have been in one hell of a hurry.

IAN: Well, as a matter of fact, she was.

MITCH: Why?

IAN: I don't think there's any point in going into that. All I can do is tell you the truth, and the truth is, I'm here with Alida. For the weekend. I'll tell you something else. I don't want to offend you but the last thing she's going to want to see when she gets back here is you.

MITCH: Is that right?

IAN: I'm afraid so.

MITCH: *(Leans in.)* What did you say your name was?

IAN: Ian.

MITCH: Well, listen carefully, Ee-yan. I just spent ninety minutes on the highway—ninety fucking minutes—

and I'm not leaving 'til I've seen my wife. Got it? *(Leans back.)* Now. Maybe it's a little unorthodox, this situation we're in here, but it's not catastrophic, is it? Is it!

IAN: No.

MITCH: You can handle it, can't you?

IAN: I think so.

MITCH: You *think* so.

IAN: I can handle it.

MITCH: Good. Then why don't you pull up a chair and sit down and stop worrying about it. Everything's going to be just fine.

   (IAN moves to the lounge chair but doesn't sit.)

What's the matter?

IAN: I'll have to ask you not to call her your wife. It makes me feel like a snake or something, and I mean, this is all above board, you know?

MITCH: Are you going to sit down now?

   (IAN sits.)

All right?

IAN: Yeah, sure. Fine.

MITCH: Good. *(Settles in.)* So. I take it this is your first time.

IAN: My first—?

MITCH: Time. Here.

IAN: Oh. Well yeah—yeah, it is. As a matter of fact. Yeah, Alida's been talking about coming up here since the day I met her, but we never quite made it. Until now.

MITCH: So what do you think?

IAN: Well, it—could use some work.

MITCH: I meant the lake.

IAN: The lake? The lake's incredible.

MITCH: You think so?

IAN: It blows me away.

MITCH: No kidding. *(Stares off.)* I hate that fucking lake.

IAN: Really? Why?

MITCH: I don't know. Association. *(Beat.)* Everything I once owned is floating in it.

IAN: What do you mean?

MITCH: Alida. Maybe I shouldn't tell you this. It was just before The Big B.U. That's French for break-up. She took everything I owned—clothes, books, photographs, you name it, everything I'd even breathed on. Piled it all up in the back yard and set a match to it. And then—and then! She hired a plane, and flew up here, and dumped all the ashes on Beautiful Lake Winnipeg!

   (IAN smiles.)

She did.

IAN: I believe you.

MITCH: And then she sent me the bill for the fucking plane.

   (IAN laughs.)

You think that's funny?

IAN: Well, I … not for you, I guess.

MITCH: That's for damn sure.

IAN: I imagine she had her reasons.

MITCH: Her what?

IAN: Her reasons, you know, I'm sure she—

MITCH: Look, are you going to tell me now? Or is it still some kind of fucking secret?

IAN: What's that?

MITCH: Where she is!

IAN: She went to see someone. Some woman who lives north of here.

MITCH: Salome?

IAN: That's it, yeah. Salome.

MITCH: Well. In that case, we'd better get ready.

(He stands.)

IAN: For what?

MITCH: For a little stormy weather.

IAN: What do you mean?

MITCH: I mean she'll be primed. She'll be flying high on home-made brandy.

(He moves to the table.)

IAN: Alida? She doesn't drink brandy.

MITCH: She does with Salome.

IAN: She never drinks brandy.

MITCH: Fine, have it your way. *(Picks up the liquor bottle, examines it.)* Say, Ee-yan. You got anything to drink around here? *(Grins.)*

IAN: Well, sure, obviously, but look, man—

MITCH: *(Slams the bottle down.)* Mitch! Mitch Mitch Mitch! For the last fucking time, don't call me man!

IAN: Why not, man? *(Quickly.)* A joke. It's a joke, all right?

MITCH: You really think you're funny, don't you?

IAN: No, I don't, not at all, I … I guess I'm a bit nervous, that's all. I mean, you may be comfortable with this situation but I can't honestly say that I am. Particularly.

MITCH: All the more reason to have a drink. Right?

IAN: There's beer in the cooler.

MITCH: *(Brandishes the bottle.)* I sort of had my eye on this.

IAN: That's not mine, it's Alida's. And I don't think—

MITCH: Good. She owes me. *(Pours a drink.)* What's the matter now?

IAN: Nothing.

MITCH: You want a beer?

IAN: I've got one. Thanks.

(MITCH moves back to the chair, sits.)

MITCH: So. Let's see if I've got this straight. You think you're going to marry my wife.

IAN: Your ex-wife.

MITCH: You really think you're going to do it.

IAN: Oh, I'm going to do it.

MITCH: Yeah, right. Does she know about this?

IAN: Of course. We're engaged.

MITCH: Engaged! That's right, you said. *(Drinks.)* When's the big day?

IAN: Well, we haven't exactly—

MITCH: Decided.

IAN: Announced it. But I don't suppose there's any harm in telling you. It's six weeks tomorrow.

MITCH: Six weeks tomorrow. Church wedding?

IAN: A church wedding.

MITCH: Flowers, cake, tuxedo—the whole business?

IAN: Why not?

MITCH: *(Deadly.)* White dress?

IAN: *(Beat.)* You're really subtle, aren't you?

MITCH: It's just a question.

IAN: I don't know.

MITCH: You don't know if she's going to wear a white dress?

IAN: I didn't ask.

MITCH: You should have. That's the kind of question you should definitely ask my wife.

IAN: I asked you to stop calling her that.

MITCH: I mean it. Ee-yan.

> *(IAN takes a long swallow of beer.)*

IAN: Okay, it's my turn now, I've got a question for you. How did you know Alida was going to be up here?

MITCH: Why?

IAN: Well, it seems odd to me. We weren't even sure, ourselves, whether we'd make it, until just before we left. Did you—drive up on spec, or what?

MITCH: I'll tell you what, Ian. I'll level with you if you level with me. Come on, you know what I'm talking about. You're not really going to marry her.

IAN: Of course I am.

MITCH: Come off it. You don't have to pull that stuff with me. I know you're screwing her, you don't have to justify it.

IAN: I'm not.

MITCH: You're not screwing her?

IAN: I'm not justifying anything!

(IAN stands, moves away.)

MITCH: You can't marry her, for fuck's sake. You don't even know her.

IAN: What do you know about it?

MITCH: You've been seeing her, what? A month, two months? A week?

IAN: Six months. Now that's it, man, I mean—I don't mean man, I mean Mitch—Mitch! No more questions, okay? I really mean that. I think if we're going to get along here, until Alida gets back, we're going to have to steer clear of certain subjects, right? Otherwise we're going to end up in trouble, and that would be stupid. Wouldn't it? Pointless. Are you listening to me?

MITCH: Sure, yeah.

IAN: Okay?

MITCH: Whatever you say.

IAN: Good. Okay, good. Great.

(IAN picks up his beer, moves down left and sits on the steps. He drinks. MITCH drinks. A beat. MITCH starts to sing a few lines from the song "Chapel of Love.")

IAN: You're not going to let up, are you.

(MITCH sings a few more lines. Then he turns and grins at IAN.)

Are you finished?

MITCH: I could be.

IAN: Good. Then maybe you'll answer my question. I asked you how you knew she'd be here.

MITCH: Oh yeah, right. She asked me.

IAN: What do you mean, she asked you?

MITCH: She asked me to come here.

IAN: She didn't ask you.

MITCH: She asked me! For the weekend.

IAN: *(Laughs.)* What is this, some kind of joke?

MITCH: *(Deadly.)* What do *you* think?

IAN: *(Beat.)* She wouldn't do that.

MITCH: She wouldn't, huh.

IAN: It's completely out of character.

MITCH: Maybe you don't know her so well.

IAN: I know her very well.

MITCH: Do you? I don't think so. I don't think you know fuck-all about my wife.

IAN: Look! If you're going to keep talking about her, for Christ's sake stop calling her your wife!

MITCH: She is my wife.

IAN: Was!

MITCH: Is. In spirit.

IAN: *(Laughs.)* Amazing. You're amazing, you know that?

MITCH: She thinks so, too.

IAN: Yeah? Well, if she thinks you're so amazing, why do you suppose she's decided to marry me.

MITCH: She hasn't.

IAN: That'll be news to her.

MITCH: You hope.

> *(IAN stands abruptly, turns away.)*

Hey, I'm not trying to offend you. Maybe you think she's going to marry you. You probably really think that. But she's not.

IAN: I can't believe this.

MITCH: Believe it. I know my wife.

IAN: *(An explosion.)* If you don't stop calling her that—

MITCH: I know my wife! And you obviously don't.

IAN: You keep saying that. You've got no business saying that. That's an incredible assumption to make.

MITCH: Is it?

IAN: Yes, it is.

MITCH: You think you know her?

IAN: I'm not saying I know everything—

MITCH: No.

IAN: I know as much as I need to know.

MITCH: Yeah? Then you should have known she asked me. Right?

> *(A beat.)*

IAN: That isn't true, I just don't buy that.

MITCH: You're calling me a liar?

IAN: If she wanted to see you—*if* she wanted to—she'd never do it here.

MITCH: Why not?

IAN: Because—shit! Because she's been talking about this frigging weekend for I don't know how long. She's been talking about coming up here, where it's nice and quiet, where nobody can get at us ... She wouldn't do it, that's all.

MITCH: She did.

IAN: She wouldn't.

MITCH: *(An explosion, on his feet.)* What's the matter with you, fuck, are you deaf, are you dumb? She asked me, she's expecting me and here—I—am!

   (Stand-off. Silence)

IAN: Once you've seen her, you go.

MITCH: Do I.

IAN: Count on it.

MITCH: *(Moves in.)*Aww. I was hoping maybe we could get something going later—the three of us, know what I mean? You up for that?

   (MITCH reaches out to touch IAN. IAN intercepts his hand and knocks it away. MITCH grins.)

IAN: There's no limit to you, is there.

MITCH: Ay, loosen up. All I'm trying to do is pass the time. We've got to pass the time, don't we? What do you want to do, play crib?

   (IAN moves down right, stares off.)

You want a drink? I'll pour.

IAN: No.

MITCH: No! *(Moves to the table.)* You're a lot of fun to be with, you know that? No wonder she asked me along for the weekend.

> *(He pours a drink.)*

IAN: Look, you know the area. I take it you know the area? Where would I find this Salome?

MITCH: Why?

IAN: I want Alida back here, now. I want this stinking mess cleared up!

MITCH: You've got a boat?

> *(He moves to the lounge chair.)*

IAN: She took the boat.

MITCH: Then you might as well forget it. You can't get there.

> *(He sits.)*

IAN: What do you mean, I can't get there?

MITCH: You can't get there.

IAN: There's no road?

MITCH: There's no road.

IAN: Maybe I can walk it.

MITCH: Nope.

IAN: Along the shore, maybe.

MITCH: I'm telling you, you can't get there by land! Got it?

> *(Beat. IAN paces.)*

IAN: This Salome. Does she have a phone?

MITCH: Do you?

IAN: Does she!

MITCH: No.

IAN: Are you sure about that?

MITCH: Nobody up here's got a fucking phone, all right? I'll tell you what you can do. You can swim it.

IAN: Really?

MITCH: You can try. Why don't you? Maybe you'll wash up sometime next spring. *(Grins.)*

IAN: Shit.

MITCH: Aw, relax, take it easy, she'll be back when she's ready. *(Beat.)* She'll be back when she's ready!

> *(IAN takes a deep breath, hesitates, then sits.)*

That's more like it. Now. Why don't we just sit here like a couple of old pals and have a nice juicy chat about my wife.

IAN: For Christ's sake, man—

MITCH: Mitch! Mitch Mitch Mitch! What do I have to do, brand it on your forehead?

IAN: You could always brand it on yours.

MITCH: You little shit—

IAN: What's the big deal, anyway? It's just an expression.

MITCH: Don't use it.

IAN: It's a habit.

MITCH: Break it!

IAN: *(Beat.)* Are you going to keep doing this?

MITCH: What?

IAN: Squandering all your charm on me.

(MITCH grins.)

MITCH: If you don't like it, you can always leave. Say! There's a motel down the highway. I'll have her call you.

IAN: Right.

MITCH: Seriously, why don't you?

IAN: Why don't I what?

MITCH: Bugger off.

(IAN faces MITCH.)

I'm just trying to save you a little embarrassment. I mean, shit, isn't it obvious? You're not wanted here. If she wanted you, she wouldn't have asked me. Right?

IAN: *If* she asked you—

MITCH: She asked me.

IAN: I'll believe that when I hear it from her.

MITCH: Suit yourself.

IAN: I will.

(He stands, starts off.)

MITCH: Where are you going now? Up down, up down, fuck. Hey! You had enough? *(Derisively.)* You leaving?

IAN: *(Turns back.)* No, I'm not leaving. I'm going to the car to get my jacket.

MITCH: Good thinking. Bring mine, while you're at it.

(MITCH throws IAN a set of keys. IAN catches them reflexively, weighs them.)

Hey, I'm parked right next to you.

(IAN starts off.)

Make sure you lock it up again. Fuck.

(IAN exits. For a moment, MITCH doesn't, moves. Then he rises, moves to the table, pours a drink, drains the glass and tosses the glass into the bushes. He moves down right, stares off. IAN returns, wearing an expensive jacket.)

(Meaning the jacket.) Hey, that's the real stuff, isn't it. Class-ee.

(IAN tosses him a light cloth jacket, takes a beer from the cooler and sits on the steps. MITCH moves next to him.)

Feel better now? Nice and warm? A little too warm, maybe. Not talking? What are you going to do, sit there and sulk?

IAN: No more talk about Alida. Okay? Do you understand?

MITCH: Like I say, if you don't like it, you can always leave.

IAN: I can't leave and you know it.

MITCH: Who's stopping you?

IAN: No more talk about Alida! Understand?

MITCH: Yeah, I understand!

IAN: Good.

MITCH: *(Leans into him.)* But I'm going to do what I damn well please. *(Pulls back.)* I always do what I damn well please. Maybe you know that. Yeah, you probably do, she probably told you. She probably told you plenty.

IAN: Wrong.

MITCH: What do you mean, wrong?

IAN: She doesn't talk about you.

MITCH: Come off it.

IAN: Ever.

MITCH: Yeah? Then tell me this. If she doesn't talk about me, what makes you so sure I'm Mitch?

IAN: *(Beat.)* What kind of a stupid question is that?

MITCH: Humor me.

IAN: *(Takes a breath.)* You said. You walked in here and you said—

MITCH: Where's Alida.

IAN: Where's Alida, I'm Mitch. What can I say, I'm brilliant.

MITCH: Don't get smart, Ee-yan. This is a serious question. Just because I said I was Mitch doesn't mean I am. I could be anyone, a complete stranger. If she never talks about me, how are you going to know?

IAN: Maybe I saw a picture, I don't know.

MITCH: A picture.

IAN: Yeah, you know, a photograph?

MITCH: She doesn't have one.

IAN: Look, what's the point of this?

MITCH: Maybe she told you what I look like. That's possible, isn't it? Did she ever tell you what I look like?

IAN: That would be a little difficult, wouldn't it. Since she never talks about you.

MITCH: Liar.

IAN: What?

MITCH: Fucking liar.

IAN: Watch it, man.

MITCH: Don't call me man!

IAN: Don't call me a liar!

MITCH: How the fuck do you know I'm Mitch!

IAN: Because you know too much.

MITCH: *(Grins.)* Very good, Ee-yan. That's just the answer I was looking for. I know too much! And don't
you forget it. *(Moves to the table, lights a candle.)* I
know all there is to know about her. All that matters.
(Suggestively.) Such as where to find her, and how to
bring her home. *(Grins.)*

IAN: Can it.

MITCH: What did I say?

IAN: Don't play dumb. That kind of talk—keep it to
yourself.

MITCH: Is that a threat? *(Moves to IAN, towers over him.)*
I think that's a threat.

> *(MITCH holds the candle over IAN's head and tips
> it slightly. IAN shifts away.)*

IAN: Knock it off.

MITCH: Are you threatening me? Ee-yan?

IAN: Get away from me, you crazy—

> *(MITCH tips the candle again; wax drips onto
> IAN's jacket. IAN knocks the candle out of
> MITCH's hand, scrambles to his feet.)*

MITCH: Come on, come on, go for it!

> *(He shoves IAN.)*

IAN: Watch it!

> *(He shoves MITCH.)*

MITCH: You watch it, punk!

IAN: Asshole!

MITCH: Come on, show me what you got. Show me what you got!

IAN: I will, I'm warning you!

MITCH: I can hardly wait.

> *(He reaches for IAN's crotch. IAN shoves him.)*

IAN: Keep your fucking hands off me!

MITCH: Whooo! Scar-ee!

> *(MITCH laughs. A beat.)*

IAN: I want to know what your game is.

MITCH: There's no game, Ee-yan. I'm just trying to keep from getting bored here. I get bored real easy, it's a problem with me.

IAN: No. There's an agenda here, I just can't figure out what it is. I put myself in your shoes—I've been sitting here trying to do that—and I can't imagine, no matter how I felt about Alida, no matter how sore or jealous I might be, I can't imagine doing to anyone what you're doing to me. You're not married to her any more, you have no claim on her, and no right— absolutely no right—to come prancing in here like you owned the place and start pounding away at me!

MITCH: Ah, don't be such a wimp.

> *(MITCH moves to the table, picks up the bottle and drinks from it. Then he grins at IAN.)*

IAN: You're an animal, you know that? No wonder you lost her.

MITCH: But I had her. Signed, sealed and delivered. Something you're never going to do.

IAN: That's what this is all about, isn't it. You're trying to scare me off.

MITCH: Awww. You've got it all figured out. Darn it! And it hardly took you any time at all.

(He sits.)

IAN: You're wasting your time. I'm not going to be driven out of here. I came here with Alida and I'm leaving with Alida. And six weeks from now, I'm going to marry Alida.

MITCH: You want to lay odds on that?

(IAN turns away in frustration.)

Hey, I'm serious about this. Fifty bucks. Fifty bucks says you never make it to the altar. Okay?

IAN: No.

(IAN moves down right.)

MITCH: Thirty, then. How about that?

IAN: I said no.

MITCH: You're scared you'll lose.

IAN: I won't lose.

MITCH: Twenty.

IAN: I can't believe this. Everything is screwed up. From the minute we got here, everything has been totally screwed up!

MITCH: Okay then—ten.

IAN: Christ, where is she! It's starting to get dark. How's she going to find her way in the dark? Maybe she's lost.

MITCH: She's not lost.

IAN: She could be.

MITCH: Not a chance. She knows this lake, grew up on it, her daddy was a fucking fisherman.

IAN: I don't like it. Anything could have happened. She could be drifting around out there. I hope she's drifting. I hope she's on the lake, not in it.

MITCH: She's not in the fucking lake, all right?

IAN: We ought to do something.

MITCH: Aw, sit down, you're making me dizzy. There's not a damn thing we can do.

IAN: We can at least worry a bit!

MITCH: You worry. I'll drink. *(Salutes him with the bottle.)* For fuck's sake, would you stop pacing?

> *(IAN stops pacing. He takes a lungful of air to calm himself.)*

Shit. You don't stand a chance, you know that? You'd never make it, even if you did marry her. You don't have the stomach for my wife.

IAN: You don't know me.

MITCH: I know her.

IAN: Yeah, you told me.

MITCH: Inside out. She's not what you'd call uncharted territory.

IAN: Oh, shut up, I've had it up to here with you.

> *(IAN sits.)*

MITCH: You don't know what's going on, do you. Still haven't figured it out. *(Leans forward.)* She staged the whole thing.

IAN: What whole thing.

MITCH: This whole thing. You don't believe me.

IAN: Is there some reason I should?

MITCH: Think about it. First she asks me up here for the weekend, only she doesn't bother mentioning it to you. That's one. Then she asks you up here. That's two. Then what? Before you can even dip your big toe in Beautiful Lake Winnipeg, she's disappeared. That's three. You get the picture?

IAN: You're crazy. *(After a moment.)* You're saying she wanted to bring us together. Why?

MITCH: You figure it out.

IAN: She wouldn't do that.

MITCH: She wouldn't, huh.

IAN: She wouldn't. She's no sadist.

MITCH: No sadist. Fuck. Are you out to lunch.

(MITCH stands, goes in search of the lantern, then sets about lighting it.)

I've got a little treat for you, Ian. I'm going to tell you a story. Are you listening to this? This goes back, I don't know—a year, maybe two years before The Big B.U. We were in Florence. You been to Florence? Firenze, Italia. Fine city, a very fine city. Not too clean, maybe. Anyway, we're there. And Alida's flying, she's at the peak of her game. I've never seen her so hot. So. One morning I wake up and she's gone—no note, no message, nothing. I'm not too concerned, not at first. I have a pretty good idea where she is. There's a spot we'd been to a couple of times, on the river, very … a very meaningful spot for both of us. So I pull on some clothes and head over there and she's been there, all right. She's left her shirt behind.

IAN: Her shirt?

MITCH: Her shirt. So now I know where she's been but I

don't know where she's gone. All I know is she's running through Firenze, Italia half naked.

IAN: You're full of it.

MITCH: Okay, let's say she's not, let's say she's covered up like a nun from head to foot. Does that make you feel better? I hunt for hours, ask about her everywhere. No one has seen her. I mean, they'd remember a woman running by with no shirt, right? Even if she's hardly got a handful. *(Grins.)* Finally I start checking out the hospitals. That's where I find her—in traction, bandages up to here. Cut up bad. You want to know what she'd done? She'd run to that spot on the river, planning to throw herself in. Started taking off her clothes—that explains the shirt, she had some idea she wanted to go down naked, I don't know. Fortunately, they wouldn't let her jump—a dozen people came running—but she managed to slip away, across this little square and into a building—a bank I think it was, only one story, that was a good thing. Ran up the stairs to the roof, dropped her skirt and jumped. Went right through the roof of the building next door, landed smack in the middle of a barber shop. Brought half the roof down with her. It was glass—did I mention that? The barber shop was a kind of lean-to affair, up against the bank, and the roof was mostly glass.

IAN: *(Beat.)* Jesus.

MITCH: You've noticed the scars. You had to notice the scars. She wouldn't tell you how she got them, right? Now you know. *(Sits.)* I'll tell you something. I'd give a lot to have seen the look on that barber's face when she came crashing through. *(Grins.)*

IAN: God, you're callous.

(IAN moves away.)

MITCH: Not callous, calloused. I've got callouses in places you don't even know about, thanks to her. *(Drinks.)* What are you staring at?

IAN: I'm not staring, I'm waiting for the point.

MITCH: The point.

IAN: There's got to be a point to the story.

MITCH: You're kidding me. You don't get it?

IAN: Why don't you spell it out for me?

MITCH: The point is she'll eat you alive! Ee-yan.

IAN: Oh, that's it. A good thing you explained it. I thought maybe you were telling me you'd made her so miserable she wanted to die.

MITCH: She didn't want to die.

IAN: She didn't even care how she did it, she was that desperate!

MITCH: Desperate, my ass. What that was—that whole breath-taking escapade—that's called Living on the Edge. You think you're up for that? Do you?

IAN: It had nothing to do with you, then. You weren't responsible in any way.

MITCH: Of course not.

IAN: I see. *(A breath.)* Look, I uh … I've got a bit of a confession to make. I said Alida never talks about you. That's not true.

MITCH: I knew it. She's always talking about me. She's obsessed with me.

IAN: Yeah. Oh yeah, I'd say so. Like, for instance … one night a few months ago, we were up here on the lake. Not here, of course, south of here. We were at a party, at this house on the beach. A fairly wild party. And after a few hours, we slipped out—went for a walk along the shore. It was something else, I'm telling you. Pitch black, and windy. Waves crashing in but you couldn't really see them, there was just this great— heaving—presence out there, pounding, throbbing ... totally out of control, you know? Very sexy. And we uh ... (*Smiles.*) I don't know if I should say this but we climbed out onto this huge flat rock that jutted out into the lake—very slippery, very wet—and we ... well, we made love there, on that rock, with the waves crashing over us. Every second in danger of being swept off and carried away, and it was—well! I have never been so scared—and so high—in my life.

MITCH: Get to the point.

IAN: What's that?

MITCH: Get to the fucking point.

IAN: Right: Well, when it was over, Alida mentioned you. She did, I'll never forget it, she said—you know, Ian. I'd never have jumped through that roof in Florence if Mitch had been half as good as you.

    (A deadly silence.)

MITCH: You little shit.

IAN: Or maybe she said nice. It's possible she said nice.

MITCH: You fucking little shit.

IAN: You'd still have her if you'd looked after her, don't you know that? You've got no one to blame but yourself!

MITCH: I looked after her!

IAN: You looked after her, all right.

MITCH: I looked after her just fine! *(Stands.)* I'm still looking after her.

IAN: Sometimes she still shakes when she's touched, did
you know that? She can't sleep in the dark, won't make
love in the light. She has nightmares that would curl
your toes. I've even seen her—

MITCH: You think you've got it all figured out, don't you?
Well, I've got news for you. You're just one of a long
line—do you understand what I'm saying? You're one
of a very long line of horny little shits who thought they
were going to save my wife! *(A beat.)* You don't
believe me. You think you're the first. Come on! A
piece like her? Hey, do they still say that? Do they still
call a woman a piece? I'm a little out of touch.

IAN: Jesus.

>*(He turns away.)*

MITCH: You're not the first young pup to come sniffing
'round my wife!

>*(A beat. MITCH moves to the table, picks up the
>liquor bottle.)*

Now. I've got one last question for you—puppy-dog.
I want to know what you did to my wife.

IAN: *(Beat.)* What *I* did to her.

MITCH: You heard me.

IAN: What's this, now?

MITCH: I think you did her in.

IAN: Did her in? *(Laughs.)* You're nuts, man.

>*(MITCH smashes the bottle against the edge of the
>table, faces IAN.)*

Christ.

>*(MITCH advances on IAN. IAN backs off.)*

MITCH: Look at it from my point of view. I come all the

way up here, expecting to find Alida. Do I find her? No. What do I find? Ee-yan! Sitting here saying the same thing, over and over. She's out. Out. *(Swings.)* Out!

IAN: She is!

MITCH: Sure she is. Jumped in a boat and took off. With a storm coming.

IAN: What storm, there's no storm.

MITCH: Didn't even stop to unlock the cottage.

IAN: Put that thing down.

MITCH: What did you do to her? *(Swings.)* Puppy-dog!

IAN: You maniac—

> *(MITCH backs IAN up against the cottage and shoves the jagged end of the bottle against his throat.)*

MITCH: Talk. Talk, or so help me—

IAN: She took off in the boat. She was mad and she took off!

MITCH: She was mad?

IAN: Yeah, mad. At me!

MITCH: Why? Talk!

IAN: We had a fight.

MITCH: Sure, you did.

IAN: We did! In the car, on the way up.

MITCH: What about!

IAN: Nothing, just a stupid—a fight, you know? You have them.

> *(A beat. MITCH grins.)*

MITCH: That's right, puppy-dog. You have them—with her.

(MITCH lowers the bottle, steps back.)

Fights, scenes, escapades, performances. Games! She needs that stuff, has to have it, she's addicted. *(Moves to the table.)* You want to spend your life feeding an addiction? *(Sets the bottle on the table, faces IAN.)* Well, do you?

IAN: *(Beat.)* At least she'll never bore me.

MITCH: I know who's going to get bored.

IAN: I don't think so.

MITCH: Before you can say puppy-love.

(IAN sinks down onto the steps.)

What Alida's got, there's no cure for. I'm telling you this for your own good. You think you can cure her but you can't. You know why? Because she doesn't want to be cured. I know. I know because I'm the same, we've got the same—inclination. Maybe you noticed that.

(Silence. MITCH opens the cooler, takes out a beer, opens it.)

IAN: Don't you think you've had enough?

MITCH: Never enough, puppy-dog. That's my motto.

(He toasts him, drinks.)

IAN: You're a bad drunk. The worst.

MITCH: *(Looks him in the eye.)* Who says I'm drunk.

(The glance holds. IAN turns away.)

Do yourself a favor, Ian. Get lost. You hear me? Go. While you can.

(IAN sits motionless, staring off.)

You're not going to, are you. Incredible. What are you, stubborn? Or just stupid.

IAN: *(From a distance.)* Oh, I'm ...

MITCH: What?

IAN: *(Faces MITCH, hesitates, shrugs.)* Curious?

(They stare at one another. Then IAN stands, moves to a suitcase, pulls out a towel, starts off.)

MITCH: Where are you going.

IAN: For a swim.

MITCH: You feel hot?

IAN: No.

MITCH: Dirty?

(MITCH laughs. IAN exits.)

Hey. Hey, Ian! Don't drown.

(Blackout.)

Scene Two

(Twenty minutes later. The clearing is in darkness; even the lantern is out. SALOME sits on the steps, shrouded in shadow. She's about 55 and has a body that once turned heads. She wears a shawl over a flamboyant dress with a plunging neckline. She holds a flashlight at her chest. IAN enters, towelling his hair.)

IAN: Mitch? You there? Who's there?

(SALOME turns on the flashlight, pointed at her chin, and grins ghoulishly.)

Jesus!

(SALOME laughs.)

Shut that off. Would you shut that off?

(SALOME does.)

Who are you?

SALOME: Light the lantern.

IAN: What?

SALOME: The lantern. It's right there by the table. *(Stands.)* Oh, never mind, I'll do it.

> *(She picks up the lantern, sets it on the table and lights it.)*

IAN: Are you going to tell me who you are?

SALOME: You don't know me?

IAN: How could I?

SALOME: I know you. Better than you might think. *(Looks him over.)* I saw you peeing in the lake.

IAN: You—

SALOME: We don't like boys who pee in our lake. Not normally. You just go right ahead and do it.

IAN: Look, who are you, anyway? And where's Mitch?

SALOME: Mitch?

IAN: Yeah, Mitch. Do you know him? He was just here.

SALOME: Here.

IAN: Twenty minutes ago.

SALOME: Right. *(Draws a flask from her pocket, uncaps it.)* I suppose you're going to want some.

IAN: No, thank you.

SALOME: It's good, made it myself. It's brandy.

> *(She drinks.)*

IAN: Salome! You're Salome, aren't you?

SALOME: *(Sings.)* "Salome, oh Salome, 'At's my girl, Salome."

IAN: Oh boy, am I glad to see you.

SALOME: "Standin' there with her bum half bare, Every little wiggle makes the boys despair."

IAN: Listen, Salome, I—

SALOME: "Every little wiggle makes the boys despair!"

IAN: *(Beat.)* I need to know where Alida is.

SALOME: *(Turns away.)* No kidding.

IAN: She took off in the boat—fifty, sixty minutes ago. She was headed for your place, but you—oh God. You haven't seen her.

SALOME: Says who?

IAN: Tonight? You've seen her tonight?

SALOME: I've seen her. And you've seen Mitch, right?

IAN: Right.

SALOME: Right! *(Leans into him.)* Mitch is a dead man. Murdered.

IAN: What are you talking about?

SALOME: Maybe you'll be a suspect, we could use a few of those. *(Laughs.)* Good one, Salome! *(With overdone authority.)* Who are you, anyway? What are you doing here? Where's Alida?

IAN: That's what I want to know! Now listen to me, listen. Did she make it to your place?

SALOME: *(Turns away.)* She lands on her feet. Like a cat.

IAN: Then she made it.

SALOME: She made it.

IAN: Thank God. Then where is she now? Where is she!

SALOME: Don't shout at me. How the hell do I know where she is?

IAN:You were just with her! Weren't you just with her?

SALOME: I was just with her.

IAN: Well then?

SALOME: I have no idea. *(Offers the flask.)* Want a nip?

(IAN spins away in frustration.)

I said do you want a nip.

IAN: No.

SALOME: No! Rude boy.

IAN: What is going on around here, would somebody please tell me? Christ!

SALOME: Profaner. Heretic.

IAN: Wait a minute. How did you get here?

SALOME: Why?

IAN: Just tell me how you got here.

SALOME: I walked.

IAN: You walked. He said you couldn't walk it. He said there was absolutely no way to get from your place to here by land.

SALOME: Who did?

IAN: Mitch!

SALOME: Mitch. Well, if you're going to talk to dead men

... *(Lets it hang; adjusts her dress.)* Tell me something, do you like my dress? It's not too much, is it?

IAN: *(Turns away.)* Incredible.

SALOME:Do you like it or not?

IAN: Forget about your dress and think about Alida!

SALOME: What about her?

IAN: Where is she!

> *(ALIDA has entered. She's about 35—slender, attractive. Her clothes are casual; over her clothes is a life jacket.)*

ALIDA: I'm right here.

> *(IAN spins around to face her.)*

And I'm in trouble.

IAN: I want to know where you've been.

ALIDA: I've been at Salome's.

IAN: All this time?

ALIDA: No. No, I've spent most of the time sitting out on that damn lake, rowing. I ran out of gas, can you believe it? *(Turns away.)* I wish you'd stop staring at me, you're making me feel like a criminal.

IAN: Alida ... I've been worried about you.

ALIDA: Well, you shouldn't have been. What's there to worry about? I keep telling you I'm too evil to die young.

IAN: No jokes, Alida. I'm telling you, I'm in no mood for jokes.

ALIDA: All right. What do you want me to say, that I'm sorry? I'm sorry. I behaved badly. Ran off and abandoned you, your first night here. But I'm back now, aren't I. Aren't I? So. Why don't you come over here and ... make me feel welcome.

(IAN hesitates, then moves to her but doesn't touch her.)

What's the matter.

IAN: You've been drinking.

ALIDA: A little brandy.

IAN: I thought you hated brandy.

ALIDA: Don't do this, Ian. Don't spoil what's left of the evening.

(He hesitates, then kisses her.)

SALOME: *(From the steps.)* Are we going to eat or what?

ALIDA: *(To IAN.)* Your lips are cold. You've been swimming.

IAN: Yes. *(Unbuckles her life jacket.)* I went for a swim, and I thought about things, and I decided to give you the benefit of the doubt.

ALIDA: I beg your pardon?

IAN: *(Removes the life jacket.)* Ask her to leave.

SALOME: What's that?

IAN: Ask her to leave, Alida.

ALIDA: I can't do that. I told her we'd feed her.

SALOME: Damn right.

IAN: I mean it, Alida.

ALIDA: What's the matter with you? I can't send her home hungry. If you could see what's in her fridge—

IAN: *(Takes her by the shoulders.)* Listen to me! We have to talk, it's important.

ALIDA: You're shaking. Why are you shaking?

IAN: *(Lets go of her.)* Jesus, Alida! *(Deep breath.)* I thought you were out there on the lake, all this time, or in it, or washed up on shore somewhere—

ALIDA: I'm fine, feel me. I'm real!

IAN: And this place. I hate to have to tell you, this is some secluded hide-away.

ALIDA: Oh well, Salome.

IAN: I'm not talking about Salome.

ALIDA: What, then?

IAN: I'm talking about Mitch.

ALIDA: *(Beat.)* Mitch.

IAN: Your charming Ex. He was here.

ALIDA: That isn't funny, Ian.

IAN: You're not kidding!

ALIDA: That isn't funny!

IAN: I didn't think it was. Especially when he smashed the whiskey bottle and went for my throat.

ALIDA: *(Backs off.)* There's something in the air tonight, can you smell it? Lunacy!

    (She runs up the steps to the door.)

IAN: Did you hear what I said!

ALIDA: *(Searches her pockets.)* Oh hell, I've lost the keys.

SALOME: Does that mean we don't get to eat?

ALIDA: Damn it anyway. *(Rattles the door, moves to the window, rattles the window.)* Wouldn't you know it? Everything's locked up tight.

IAN: Alida—

ALIDA: *(Moves to the steps.)* Never mind, I'll think of something. But first I know what I need. I need a drink! *(Moves down the steps to the table, picks up the broken bottle.)* My whiskey. *(Faces IAN.)* Is this what's left of my whiskey?

IAN: I just finished telling you—

ALIDA: Ian! A brand new bottle.

IAN: Oh, great. Terrific. I'm lucky I'm here at all, and you're whining about a bottle.

ALIDA: It's not just a bottle, and you know it.

IAN: Well, if it makes you feel any better, he drank it first.

ALIDA: Who did?

IAN: Mitch! *(Moves to her, takes the bottle.)* Now listen to me, listen! We have to talk about this.

SALOME: I say we eat first.

IAN: Butt out, Salome.

SALOME: You butt out!

IAN: *(To ALIDA.)* We have to talk about Mitch!

SALOME: Mitch is dead! I told you that already, what's the matter with you, don't you understand plain English?

    (A beat. IAN turns from SALOME back to ALIDA.)

ALIDA: He is. *(With a strange little laugh.)* He's dead.

SALOME: He was murdered.

ALIDA: He wasn't murdered—

SALOME: He was murdered.

ALIDA: *(To IAN.)* He drowned. Out there. Four years ago.

(With a flourish.) So I don't know who was here but it wasn't Mitch, was it?

(She moves away.)

IAN: *(Beat.)* You never told me he was dead.

ALIDA: No?

IAN: No.

ALIDA: Well, I suppose you never asked.

IAN: It's not the sort of thing you ask, it's the sort of thing people volunteer.

ALIDA: Do they.

IAN: They do, yeah. They mention it, in passing.

ALIDA: But I never talk about him, you know that.

IAN: Alida, for Christ's sake—

ALIDA: I know. You don't think it's true, but why not? People die all the time, why not him? He could have.

IAN: *(Beat.)* All right. How?

ALIDA: I told you, he drowned.

IAN: How?

ALIDA: How do people usually drown?

IAN: *(A warning.)* Alida—

ALIDA: All right! He was fishing. He was out there, alone, in a boat, fishing, and … something happened.

IAN: What?

ALIDA: He was alone in the boat! *(Sits.)* It was just at breakup, when the water is—mercifully cold. He would have died the second he hit the water, and then he'd have gone out with the ice. Who knows how far he got—Hudson Bay, Baffin Bay, Iceland. So that was good, he always liked to travel. *(Glances at IAN.)* A joke, Gloompot.

SALOME: The boat washed up north of here. Without oars.

ALIDA: Salome—

SALOME: I don't care, I'm suspicious.

ALIDA: Well, anyway. That's how he went. Lake Winnipeg got him, and I say good for Lake Winnipeg.

SALOME: Amen to that. *(Drinks.)*

IAN: *(Trying to stay cool.)* Why are you doing this?

ALIDA: You asked me, you wanted to know.

IAN: You're pulling that stuff again—flying off into fantasyland! I'm telling you, Alida, this is no time for that.

ALIDA: *(Flaring.)* Well, if you don't like it then for God's sake stop talking to me about Mitch!

IAN: Listen to me. You can't just pretend it didn't happen, I'm not going to let you do that. He was here—

ALIDA: No.

IAN: He was here, with me, tonight. Now that's a fact, you can't wish it away. And, Alida, you know what he said? He said that you'd—

ALIDA: *(Stands.)* I won't listen to this! I've been on the lake for nearly an hour—rowing in the dark—and I'm sick of my own thoughts and I'm starving! I don't suppose you thought to start the barbecue.

IAN: The barbecue.

ALIDA: It didn't occur to you I might be a little hungry when I got back?

IAN: I guess not.

ALIDA: Nice.

IAN: I've had other things on my mind.

ALIDA: Obviously.

IAN: Are we going to fight about this now?!

ALIDA: Not if you do as you're told!

> *(IAN turns and hurls the broken bottle against the cottage.)*

SALOME: Hey! Watch it.

IAN: *(To ALIDA.)* You've got ten seconds.

ALIDA: *(Beat.)* Yes, all right. He's not dead.

SALOME: Alida!

ALIDA: He's not, Salome.

SALOME: Since when?

ALIDA: *(To IAN.)* It's just a story we invented, because I wanted him dead so badly. I wished him dead, I willed him dead ... and one day he was.

SALOME: What are you saying? It's no story.

ALIDA: We extinguished him, Salome, remember? *(Touches her temple.)* Up here. *(Turns away from SALOME.)* What a relief. To have one small place in the world where he didn't exist.

SALOME: I don't get this. I don't get this at all.

ALIDA: *(To IAN.)* Ignore her, she's plastered.

SALOME: Liar.

ALIDA: That's enough out of you. I think you'd better go home.

SALOME: Without eating?

ALIDA: We're locked out, Salome.

SALOME: Well—can't we break in?

ALIDA: No, we can't break in! We've got to find the keys. Maybe you can do that, can you? Can you look for them?

SALOME: Where?

ALIDA: The boat. Check the boat, and all along the path to the dock. Take your flashlight. *(Sweet reason.)* If you find them, then we can eat, can't we?

SALOME: I don't see why I have to do all the grub work.

> *(SALOME exits, with the flashlight. A few beats.)*

ALIDA: I wish you wouldn't look at me like that.

IAN: Like what.

ALIDA: Like you don't know whether to hug me or hit me.

IAN: I don't understand you. I don't understand why you'd try to pretend the guy is dead.

ALIDA: She started it. She started saying he was dead and I just ... *(Catches herself; takes a beat.)* Right. Sorry. It was wishful thinking, that's all. When it comes to Mitch, I do a lot of that. Is that so terrible? Oh, God. He was really here, wasn't he. Why?

IAN: He said you'd invited him.

ALIDA: He would.

IAN: You didn't?

ALIDA: *(Faces him; takes a beat.)* I beg your pardon?

IAN: Reassure me.

ALIDA: *(Stands.)* I will not.

IAN: Thanks.

ALIDA: *(Moves away.)* I'm not going to play into his hand.

IAN: Forget him, it's me you're dealing with here!

ALIDA: I won't play into yours either. You don't deserve it, you're as bad as he is.

IAN: Thanks again.

ALIDA: Oh, this is wonderful, this is. A fine way to start a marriage. Plant a seed and watch it grow!

IAN: *(Sighs.)* Alida—I didn't really believe him.

ALIDA: You sure as hell did, it's written all over you.

IAN: *(An explosion.)* I'm still here, aren't I! Now I told you when you got back, when you finally got back here—what did I say to you? *(Moves to her, takes her arms.)* I said I'd gone for a swim and thought about things, and I'd decided to give you the benefit of the doubt. Didn't I!

ALIDA: That's supposed to make me feel better?!

> *(IAN lets go of her, turns away.)*

Why would I invite him, for heaven's sake? What reason would I have? What reason did he give?

IAN: Business.

ALIDA: Business?

IAN: First he said something about some business that had to be cleared up. And then later he ... he implied that you wanted me to meet him.

ALIDA: You must be joking.

IAN: He went to quite a bit of trouble to convince me that marrying you would be an adventure about on a par with swallowing cyanide.

ALIDA: Oh, I get it. Yes, I'm starting to get the picture now. He's been telling you stories, hasn't he. Filling your ears with fantasies! What did he tell you? No, let me guess. Florence! He told you about Florence, didn't he. How I went running through Firenze, Italia stark naked—or did he allow me a skirt, it varies—and jumped through a roof and scarred myself in several significant places. Did he tell you about that?

IAN: Yes.

ALIDA: Why not? It's easily his most engrossing lie. But you believed him.

IAN: Not exactly.

ALIDA: What does that mean!

IAN: I believe it happened. Not the way he tells it.

ALIDA: You think I go around jumping off roofs.

IAN: You've got the scars to prove it.

ALIDA: I've got scars, what does that prove.

IAN: Then you didn't jump off a roof?

ALIDA: There you go again! *(Moves to the table, slams fist down.)* Oh, what I wouldn't give for a drink!

(A few beats. ALIDA gets herself in hand.)

Ian. Don't you see what he was trying to do?

IAN: Oh, I see it, I think. The question is, why.

ALIDA: Who knows. Maybe he was bored. *(Takes a breath.)* When he was a boy—now this is a true story. His father was a cop, and when Mitch was a boy, he used to sneak his father's revolver out of the holster and run off to some pasture with it, and put one bullet in the chamber and point the gun here *(Points a finger at her temple.)* and pull the trigger. He did! Often. Do you want to know how he explained that kind of behavior? He said he was so bored with life that he needed the possibility of dying to keep from killing himself. That's what he said, you figure it out. He's a madman. And there's something else. He's terribly possessive, always was. He's never really got it through his head that I'm not his, anymore. He's obsessed with me.

IAN: That's funny. He said the same thing about you.

ALIDA: And what do you think. Am I?

IAN: I hope not, Alida.

ALIDA: *(Beat.)* No one could ever accuse *you* of dishonesty.

> *(She turns away. Silence.)*

IAN: Look, I don't want to fight about it anymore. You know how I feel about you—

ALIDA: How do you feel about me?

IAN: What kind of a question is that?

ALIDA: Tell me, I need to know.

IAN: I'm going to marry you, aren't I?

ALIDA: You're crazy about me.

IAN: *(Smiles.)* I can take you or leave you.

ALIDA: *(Faces him.)* I make you crazy. I make you so crazy sometimes, you'd like to crush me. Say it.

IAN: You make me crazy.

ALIDA: Do you love me?

IAN: Yes.

ALIDA: Trust me?

IAN: In what way? *(Beat.)* Okay, I don't completely trust you. So what. I made that trade-off months ago. Don't look at me like that, you know what I'm talking about. I *had* someone I trusted completely, and I left her, didn't I. I left her for you, Alida.

ALIDA: Why don't you trust me?

IAN: Well, for one thing, because of the gaps.

ALIDA: The gaps.

IAN: The gaps in your history, the things you won't talk about. Like Mitch. You refuse to discuss him—or if you do, I can't tell what's fact and what's fiction. You have secrets from me, Alida. So you can hardly blame me for listening—for at least listening—when someone comes along who starts to fill in the gaps.

ALIDA: *(Beat.)* All right, I see what you mean. You have a point there. I don't mean to have secrets, it's just— you know. Necessary, if you're going to be A Woman Of Mystery. *(Glances at him.)* Sorry. Not funny. *(Moves to him.)* Oh, Ian. Don't let him come between us. Please.

IAN: All right. *(Kisses her.)* I'm sorry.

ALIDA: That's not sorry. This is sorry.

> *(She kisses him seductively. SALOME enters, up center, with an axe.)*

SALOME: Whore.

> *(ALIDA and IAN pull apart.)*

ALIDA: *(Irritably.)* Back already. Did you find them?

SALOME: *(Beat.)* Oh shit.

ALIDA: You forgot to look.

SALOME: No, I didn't forget to look. They're not there.

(Hoists the axe.) But anyway, I got this.

ALIDA: What for?

SALOME: We're going to break down that door.

ALIDA: No, we're not.

SALOME: We sure as hell are.

ALIDA: *(An explosion.)* Nobody's taking an axe to my cottage! Do you understand me?

> *(ALIDA strides to SALOME and grabs the axe.)*

Do you?

> *(SALOME shrugs. ALIDA turns to IAN.)*

I'll be right back.

> *(She starts off.)*

IAN: Where are you going?

ALIDA: To find my keys.

IAN: No, you're not. *(Intercepts her.)* You're not going anywhere while he's around.

ALIDA: What are you talking about? He must be gone by now.

IAN: I'm afraid not. *(Draws MITCH's keys from a pocket.)* I've got the keys to his truck.

ALIDA: Oh.

IAN: So I don't know where he is but he hasn't gone far.

ALIDA: I see. *(Rallies.)* Well—too bad!

> *(She starts off. IAN catches her.)*

IAN: Alida, just a minute. I don't want you wandering around out there in the dark.

ALIDA: I'll take the flashlight.

IAN: That's not the point. I'll go.

ALIDA: You don't know the way.

IAN: We'll both go.

ALIDA: What do you think he's going to do—creep up behind me and murder me? If he didn't do that in eight years of marriage, he's not going to do it now. Besides. *(Hoists the axe.)* I'm kind of handy with an axe.

IAN: I don't know how you can joke about this.

ALIDA: We have to find the keys, Ian.

IAN: Maybe we should just clear out. Go back to town.

ALIDA: If we did that, we'd be playing right into his hand. We can't do that. We've got to show him he can't get to us. That's the only way we can beat him, don't you understand that?

IAN: *(Beat.)* I suppose.

ALIDA: If it makes you feel any better, I'll take Salome with me. All right? In the meantime, know what you can do? Make a hungry girl happy. *(Kisses him.)* Start the barbecue.

IAN: *(Reluctantly.)* Where is it?

ALIDA: Back of the cottage. Go, Gloompot.

IAN: *(Starts off.)* How long will you be?

ALIDA: Ten minutes.

> *(IAN exits. ALIDA turns to SALOME, who is sitting on the steps, with her flask.)*

What's the meaning of this?

SALOME: Of what?

ALIDA: *(Indicating the axe.)* A bit obvious, don't you think?

(SALOME shrugs.)

Okay, give it here.

SALOME: What?

ALIDA: The brandy, Salome.

SALOME: Forget it.

ALIDA: Come on, you're already three sheets to the wind.

SALOME: That's a lie.

(ALIDA grabs the flask.)

Let go. Let go or I'll scream!

ALIDA: *(Lets go, stands back.)* That does it. You're finished.

(ALIDA picks up the flashlight and starts off. SALOME stands, follows her.)

SALOME: What do you mean, finished?

ALIDA: *(Turns back.)* Finished.

SALOME: No, I'm not. You can't do that. I don't like the way you treat me, that's all. I'm not dirt under your feet. And I don't like being the one who's stupid and dispensable and—sexless!

ALIDA: You're finished.

SALOME: Now? This minute?

ALIDA: Of course not. You've got work to do. And Salome ... *(Draws a nail file from her pocket and leans in.)* Do you see this?

SALOME: I'm not blind.

ALIDA: What is it?

SALOME: A nail file.

ALIDA: Spoil this for me, and I'll ram it up your nose. *(Draws back.)* Remember that.

> *(ALIDA pockets the nail file and exits, with the axe and the flashlight. For a moment, SALOME doesn't move.)*

SALOME: Ram it up your own nose. Whore.

> *(SALOME drinks. Blackout.)*

Scene Three

> *(Twenty minutes later. IAN sits in the lounge chair, lost in thought; his thoughts aren't pleasant. Neither are SALOME's. She's on the steps, with her flask. Finally, IAN rouses himself, checks his watch.)*

IAN: She should be back. She should have been back ten minutes ago.

> *(IAN stands, moves down right, takes a deep breath, stares off.)*

God, this place is really something, isn't it. This lake. Especially when the wind's up. I wish it was up now. *(Looks up at the sky.)* Look, Salome. The gods are showering.

> *(SALOME looks up, scowls.)*

I know what you think. You think that's Northern Lights, but you're wrong. The gods are showering, behind their luminescent shower curtains.

> *(No response. He faces her.)*

How come so quiet? You can talk to me, you know. They can't hear.

SALOME: Who?

IAN: The gods. How can they hear when they're showering?

> *(He smiles. She turns away. He moves to the steps
> and sits next to her.)*

Look, Salome, I'm sorry. I thought you were going
with Alida, I was counting on that, and when I came
back and you were still here, I just—I guess I exploded.
I shouldn't have done that. Will you accept my
apology?

> *(SALOME shrugs.)*

Good. Because I don't see any reason why you and I
can't be friends.

SALOME: *(Beat.)* You want to be friends.

IAN: That's right.

SALOME: With me.

IAN: Well, sure.

SALOME: I'll bet you do.

IAN: I do.

SALOME: Well, I'm sorry to disappoint you but I don't
want a friend. I'll tell you what I do want. I want a
lover. Wanna be my lover, lover?

IAN: *(Smiles.)* What is this?

SALOME: A proposal.

IAN: I'm already engaged.

SALOME: A proposition, then.

IAN: Come on, this is crazy talk.

SALOME: Look, I don't have all night. Are you game or
not?

IAN: Not.

SALOME: Fine. *(Stands.)* Then don't come weedling around me, talking about shower curtains in the sky and grinning that silly grin, because it won't do you a bit of good. I wasn't born yesterday. I know what you want from me, and it's not friendship.

> *(SALOME moves away, uncaps her flask, drinks.)*

IAN: You're not that jaded, are you? There has to be a motive behind everything?

SALOME: Doesn't there?

IAN: *(Beat.)* Okay, maybe you're right. Maybe I am after something here—a little help. I thought, since you're a friend of Alida's—

SALOME: I'm not her friend.

IAN: Come on, Salome.

SALOME: I'm not her friend! And even if I was, what makes you think I'd want to help you? Why should I? What are you going to do for me, if I do? Huh?

IAN: Not much, I guess.

SALOME: Right. Story of my life.

> *(SALOME moves to the lawn chair, sits.)*

IAN: That's it, then. That's your answer? Terrific.

> *(He stands, moves abruptly down right, stares off. She watches him.)*

SALOME: I don't know what you see in her, anyway. I don't know what anyone sees in *her*.

IAN: You don't know her, I guess.

SALOME: I know her.

IAN: You can't.

SALOME: I know her! Like a daughter. *(Beat.)* I raised her.

IAN: *(Beat.)* What do you mean, you raised her.

SALOME: I raised her.

IAN: What about her father? Where was he while you were raising Alida?

SALOME: As far away as we could keep him.

IAN: No, see—that's not right. I know it's not right because I know about her father, that's one person she's always talked about. She's always said how close they were, how—

SALOME: Close?

IAN: —she'd—run down to shore every day after school, to watch for his boat. And the minute she'd see it, she'd—run straight home, to fix his supper—

SALOME: She told you that? She lied. She couldn't even peel a spud 'til she was twenty. And she didn't watch for him, not once, I can tell you that. I'm the one who raised her, and I'll tell you something. She was a horrible kid.

IAN: *(Turns away.)* Here we go.

SALOME: She was horrible!

IAN: Alida's right, there's something in the air tonight.

SALOME: You know what kind of kid she was? I'll tell you. The kind that cuts worms in half and feeds the pieces to babies. And snips the nipples off kittens to see if they'll bleed. I mean it. And one time—this was the year the lake was so low, I'll never forget it. She spent three days catching frogs, you know why? So she could run spikes through them and chart how long it took them to die!

IAN: What is it about this place? Everybody's got some kind of sick, twisted story to tell about the person who just left!

SALOME: You don't believe me. You will.

(SALOME drinks. A beat.)

IAN: If you know her so well, I guess you know about her scars. Well?

SALOME: What about them?

IAN: I guess you know how she got them. Come on, you raised her. Like a daughter!

SALOME: I know, don't worry.

IAN: Go ahead, I'm waiting.

SALOME: I know.

IAN: I wonder. *(He moves to her.)* Here's another question for you. Listen carefully. If a person runs out of gas between your place and here, and has to row back, and if it takes nearly an hour to do it, how far is it from your place to here? Come on, Salome, you know the answer.

(Silence. He turns away.)

Never mind, I know it, too. What I don't know is this. Why would a person spend nearly an hour rowing between your place and here, when they could walk it in a few minutes? No, that's not the question. The question is, why would a person *say* they'd spent nearly an hour rowing—in the dark—to get from your place to here, when it couldn't possibly be true?

(He moves back to her.)

You see, Salome, I don't know what's going on around here but I sure know something is. If you'd help me— give me one little clue—I'd be all right, I could take it from there.

SALOME: Stuff it.

IAN: Stuff it. Great. Thank you, Salome, I'm in your debt
forever.

(*IAN steps back, checks his watch.*)

Half an hour. That's it, we're going after her.

SALOME: Forget it.

IAN: Come on. I'll drag you if I have to.

SALOME: Don't you touch me.

IAN: I need you to show me the way, Salome. Aw, don't
do this, don't make me force you.

SALOME: I'd like to see you force me. I'd like to see you
try!

(*IAN grabs SALOME and begins to haul her off.*)

Let go! Let go of me!

(*They struggle.*)

Goddamnit, why don't you just do what you're supposed to do!

IAN: And what's that?

SALOME: Wait here! That's the way she set it up, that's
how she wants it to go. So why don't you stop whining
about it and let it happen the way it's supposed to
happen!

(*IAN lets go of her. A beat.*)

IAN: Oh God. Oh God, Salome, don't say that. I was—
hoping ...

(*He turns away.*)

SALOME: Yeah, well, I don't care, I don't give a darn.
Serves her right. Serves you right, too. If you'd just

make yourself useful! For instance, there's supper. God knows, we've waited long enough for a bit of food. Why don't you look after that, huh? Why don't you do something worth doing? *(Beat.)* You're not going to, are you. Of course not. I can see who's going to have to do it—me! As usual. *(Moves to the table, rummages through the bags.)* Or listen to her whine about her stomach. If there's one thing I can't stand, it's people whining about their stomachs!

(The rummaging becomes an exercise in futility. She sinks down onto the steps. A few beats.)

That bit I mentioned, about the frogs? She didn't do that. It was me, did that. Okay? It was me. *(Laughs.)* What a brat. *(Sobers up.)* I'm not stupid, though. Are you listening to me? Maybe I act like I am, once in a while, but I'm not. I'm a lot smarter than her.

(Suddenly ALIDA stumbles on, covered with blood. She carries a bottle of wine.)

ALIDA: Ian?

IAN: My God.

ALIDA: Look at me, what a mess. *(A strange laugh.)* Ian? Sweetheart?

(Three beats. Blackout. End of Act One.)

Act Two

Scene One

(Ten forty-five. Moonlight, crickets, etc. Another lantern and various candles have been lit. ALIDA sits in the lawn chair, wearing a terry-cloth robe and a towel around her head. IAN enters, down left, carrying a barbecue fork and a steak on a paper plate. He tosses the fork on the table, moves to ALIDA and hands her the plate.)

ALIDA: That's it? Meat?

> *(IAN stares at her until her glance shifts.)*

> If it's the best you can do. *(Takes the plate.)* Aren't you having any?

IAN: I've lost my appetite.

ALIDA: I'll need a knife and fork.

IAN: Oh? Why?

ALIDA: Very funny. *(Beat.)* What are you staring at?

IAN: I've never seen a murderer before. An axe murderer, to boot.

ALIDA: Well? How do I look?

IAN: Fraudulent.

(ALIDA stands abruptly, moves to the table, rummages.)

ALIDA: Damn. Every damn thing's locked up inside.

IAN: Too bad you didn't find the keys.

ALIDA: That's for sure.

IAN: Did you look?

ALIDA: Of course I looked.

IAN: Before or after you hacked him up?

ALIDA: I don't remember.

IAN: I'll bet you don't.

(ALIDA picks up the barbecue fork, weighs it, drops it, then tosses the plate on the table.)

ALIDA: I guess I've lost mine, too.

IAN: *(Deadly.)* Eat it.

ALIDA: I beg your pardon?

IAN: Eat it or I'll shove it down your throat.

ALIDA: I'm not hungry!

IAN: *(Moves to her.)* Oh yes you are, you're starving, you've been crying for your supper all night long. *(Picks up the steak, shoves it under her nose.)* Well, I cooked it. Just the way you like it, see? See the blood oozing from the center? Now you—eat it!

(ALIDA knocks the plate out of his hand.)

Alida, so help me—

ALIDA: It slipped! What a shame. There's blood all over your nice designer clothes.

IAN: If you don't start leveling with me—

ALIDA: I am levelling with you!

IAN: Good. *(Grabs her hand.)* In that case, there's a body, right?

> *(He begins to pull her off.)*

ALIDA: What are you doing?

IAN: We're going to find it.

ALIDA: No!

IAN: Yes!

ALIDA: No! No, Ian, I can't, I can't go back there! Ian, please!

> *(ALIDA breaks free.)*

Stop staring at me. I can't go back and look at him. For God's sake, what do you think I'm made of?

IAN: I don't know, Alida. I'm really beginning to wonder.

> *(IAN moves to the lawn chair and sits. ALIDA rips the towel from her hair—which is damp—and tosses it aside.)*

ALIDA: I don't know what's got into you, I really don't. I must say I'm disappointed. I think, after what I've been through, I deserve a little sympathy, or something. *(Shudders.)* What's the matter with me, can't seem to stop shaking. *(Turns back to the table, picks up the wine bottle.)* Where did this come from? My God! I brought it with me, didn't I? From Salome's. But when did I pick it up? Before? After? Strange, I can't remember a thing.

> *(She picks up a corkscrew, begins to uncork the wine. Suddenly, she stops. It's as if a piece of the puzzle falls into place.)*

Yes, I can! I can remember the look on his face when

I hit him. So surprised! There were words just forming on his lips ... lost forever. *(Sighs, a little too dramatically.)* Well. They probably all started with "f," anyway.

> *(She glances at IAN, then crosses to him with the wine and the corkscrew.)*

Ian? Gloompot? Would you do the honours?

IAN: A woman who can kill a man with an axe ought to be able to open her own wine.

ALIDA: I'd rather you did it for me.

IAN: Or maybe I've got that wrong. Maybe you didn't kill him, maybe he was already dead. Maybe he drowned, in Beautiful Lake Winnipeg! Took the underwater route to Iceland.

ALIDA: You're being bitchy. It doesn't suit you.

IAN: No, wait a minute. That's wrong too, that's just wishful thinking. He didn't drown, he's alive and well. Charming as ever! He damn near charmed the pants off me—did I mention that yet? Oh yeah, take it from me, the man can perform. Question is, what was the point? What exactly was the point of the performance, and where is he now? I'd like to know that, too, because I've got the keys to his truck and I'm starting to think they'd look real good tangled up around his tonsils!

ALIDA: You're not going to, are you.

IAN: I'm going to try!

ALIDA: I meant the wine, silly.

> *(IAN grabs the wine, leaps to his feet, prepares to throw the wine violently off right, but ALIDA grabs his arm.)*

No, no, no, not the wine! Ian!

(He lets her pull the wine from his hand.)

You'd like it to be me, wouldn't you? You'd like to pick me up and hurl me against the rocks, smash me to pieces. Maybe before the night's out, you'll do that. Will you? *(Moves in tight.)* If you do, if you decide to dash my brains out on those rocks over there, you know what? I'll understand. Even as I'm hurtling through the air, in that split second before my skull cracks open, I'll know the emotion that drove you to it. And in a funny kind of way, I'll rejoice. Because I'll know we were meant for each other.

(Five beats. Nobody moves.)

IAN: Christ. *(Deep breath.)* You're a monster.

ALIDA: *(Touches him.)* That's not what you said last night. In the dark, between the sheets. Remember?

(IAN moves abruptly away.)

Now you act as though I'm diseased—liable to contaminate you. It's not fair. I did it for you, Ian.

IAN: Did what, exactly?

ALIDA: Killed him!

IAN: You shouldn't have bothered.

(ALIDA doesn't seem to hear this; another piece of the puzzle has just fallen into place.)

ALIDA: That's right! It *was* for you. It was *you* we were fighting about! *(Begins to enjoy it.)* I opened the door and he—loomed up, out of the shadows. For a split second, I didn't recognize him at all. And then immediately, automatically, we began to fight. He wouldn't back down, would not back down. I ran outside, he followed. And then, out of the blue, it hit me: I am tired—bone tired—of fighting with this man. And in the same second I felt the weight of the axe in my hand

and so I ... swung it. So natural, so easy, like falling into bed.

(ALIDA remembers the wine, sits, begins to uncork it.)

It won't do, though, will it. The truth never does do, it's never quite good enough, thank God. So. *(Beat.)* He came along and asked if he could borrow the boat, to go fishing. I agreed, why not? Old time's sake. Hours went by, days. He never returned. Scratch one much-loved boat. *(Finishes uncorking the wine.)* The only thing is, we'd have to take it out—now, while it's dark—and set it adrift. Then swim back, and bury the body. Ugh.

(She lifts the bottle and drinks from it, wiping her mouth with the back of her hand.)

Or. He showed up unexpectedly at Salome's, found us together, came at you in a jealous rage. A struggle—terrible. Being younger, and happening to have an axe, you killed him. *(Glances at IAN.)* Or I did, if you like. He was on top of you, strangling you, I had to do something, I grabbed what came to hand. Lucky it was an axe, lucky it was sharp. *(Beat.)* Not bad. Plausible, and not too original. They don't like it if you're too original. On the whole, I like the first one best. *(Beat.)* Yes, definitely. I'll get Salome to bury him.

(ALIDA drinks again. IAN, who has been watching her, now strides across to her and takes the bottle from her hand.)

IAN: Okay, you've had your little performance, now it's my turn. I don't know what the hell's going on here, but I know this much. You didn't kill Mitch, so you can stop pretending you did.

ALIDA: I came stumbling in here, covered with blood!

IAN: Forget it, we're not going to talk about it, we're going to talk about *us*. You're going to give me some answers, now, finally! Are you reading me?

ALIDA: Give me the wine.

IAN: No.

ALIDA: Give me the wine, Ian.

IAN: No.

ALIDA: No wine, no answers.

> *(IAN hands her the wine.)*

IAN: Are you ready now?

ALIDA: Yes.

IAN: Are you sure you're ready?

ALIDA: Hit me.

IAN: You knew Mitch was coming here tonight. You knew it all along. *(Leans in.)* How! How did you know?

ALIDA: How do you think?

IAN: You invited him?

ALIDA: Not exactly.

IAN: What the hell does that mean!

ALIDA: Don't shout at me. I'll clam right up if you shout at me.

IAN: Did you invite him, or didn't you?

ALIDA: Let's put it this way. I knew he was coming and I knew what he was coming for. All right? Is that what you want to hear? But we had fight, Ian. Over you. He wanted to go too far, so I killed him. You don't believe me, but I did, I really killed him, and I'm not sorry. What did he amount to anyway, what was he? An

expert on cruelty—and venereal disease. That's another story. I killed him, and what's more I enjoyed it.
That's what marriage does for you, you see? Teaches
you what true hatred is!

IAN: *(Trying to stay calm.)* Why did you let him come
here? Alida?

ALIDA: Why? To save you.

IAN: From what?

ALIDA: From me.

IAN: *(Moves away.)* Oh no you don't, you're not starting
that.

ALIDA: I've tried and tried to tell you, but you won't—

IAN: Right, you've got it.

ALIDA: Listen to me, listen! I'd like to be what you think
I am—I'd transform myself if I could—but it's not
possible. Ian, listen. What you see when you look at
me—that's a lie. The exterior is a lie. There you go,
there you go again, you always turn away! *(Beat.)* I'm
greedy, that's the trouble—a real pig. And restless,
too. Not much good to anyone, including myself. And
inside my head—here, where it matters—there's a war
going on, a trench war. Blood and guts and rats and
muck—

IAN: Stop it.

ALIDA: Even in my sleep I can—

(*IAN grabs her by the shoulders.*)

IAN: Alida, just—stop it!

(*A beat. He lets go.*)

Why do you do that to yourself?

ALIDA: You don't believe me. For God's sake, shouldn't

I know?

IAN: No! You're the last person who should know. You spend so much time flipping in and out of reality, you don't know what's real anymore. But I do, Alida. I do! Now. I want you to tell me why you let this happen. I want the truth, no matter what it is.

ALIDA: He made me.

IAN: *(Explosively.)* I knew it! I knew he was at the bottom of this. If I ever get my hands on that son-of-a-bitch, I'll kill him.

ALIDA: I've already done that.

IAN: *(Moving, excited.)* So. So! He put you up to this. He made you invite me up here so that he could—what? Scare me off?

ALIDA: Yes.

IAN: Why?

ALIDA: Because he's jealous.

IAN: He still wants you. Or maybe he doesn't really want you but he doesn't want anyone else to have you.

ALIDA: He wants me. He always wants me.

IAN: So. He phones you up—is this how it goes? He phones you up?

ALIDA: What does it matter?

IAN: I need to know this, Alida.

ALIDA: He phones me up.

IAN: Says do me a favour, will you—big favour. Get that boyfriend of yours, that fiancé—did he know I was your fiancé?

ALIDA: No.

IAN: No. Never mind. Get him in the car, get him up to the cottage—then clear out for a while, so I can ... so I can ... *(Beat.)* And you said ... *(Another beat; faces her.)* What did you say, Alida?

ALIDA: God, you turn me on.

IAN: What did you say!

ALIDA: You really do, you know?

IAN: Alida, I think you should know I'm just about at the end of my—

ALIDA: I wanted to tell you, I really wanted to, I wanted to warn you! That's the truth, Ian. I couldn't.

IAN: Why not?

ALIDA: You don't know him. You don't know what he's capable of.

IAN: You're afraid of him?

ALIDA: Yes! Yes yes yes, don't you understand anything?

IAN: It's more than fear, though, isn't it. It goes a lot deeper than that. He's done a number on you—got you all twisted up. He's got you convinced you're not fit for anyone but him, not for anyone decent. God knows, we've been through that often enough. So naturally ... when he makes this phone call you'd obviously ... *(Trails off; moves down right.)* No. It doesn't wash.

ALIDA: *(Beat.)* He did make me do it. Only not the way you think.

IAN: How?

ALIDA: By knowing me too well. By knowing my worst fears and exploiting them. I told you, he's a madman, but clever. He doesn't care about anyone but himself and he—knows things about people that are ... secret, secret things. He sniffs them out, don't ask me how. He does. *(Begins to enjoy it.)* Like that time in Peru, we were in Peru I think it was, and there was this river—full of life, teeming, crawly, scaley—and he knew the one thing I could never, ever do was jump in that river, even to put my finger in it meant—pure panic. And so, naturally, that's what I had to do. I had to jump in. He made me, you see? By knowing that I'd rather die than do it. *(Winds down.)* But it wasn't always him. In the same way I've made him do things, go places he was scared of. Oh, yes. Lots of those.

IAN: Such as?

ALIDA: Such as? Oh, you know—suburbia. Shopping malls. Backyards.

IAN: This is another one, isn't it? This is just another goddamn fantasy! *(Sits; stares off.)* Christ, Alida. If you didn't want to marry me, all you had to do was say so.

ALIDA: But I do want to marry you.

IAN: I'd noticed.

ALIDA: *(Moves to him.)* I can't stand the thought of anyone else having you. *(Runs a finger along his spine.)* That's the same thing, isn't it?

IAN: I can't believe a word you say, you know that? *(Faces her.)* Do you know what that's like!

ALIDA: Kiss me.

IAN: No.

ALIDA: Please.

IAN: No.

ALIDA: I'll die if you don't. I swear to God, I'll die right here at your feet.

IAN: I wish you would, you know that? I almost wish you

would.

ALIDA: Please.

IAN: Alida—

ALIDA: Please please please.

IAN: I can't believe the stuff I let you get away with.

(She kisses him seductively; then he holds her off.)

No more lies, Alida.

ALIDA: More.

IAN: No more lies, okay? I want the truth.

ALIDA: I want your mouth.

IAN: Alida—

ALIDA: Gimme, gimme, gimme.

(She kisses him again. He gives into it for a moment, then starts to pull away.)

IAN: No. No. What are you doing? Leave me alone.

ALIDA: What's the matter?

IAN: Get away from me.

ALIDA: Ian—

IAN: Get away from me so I can think! I mean it, Alida.

(She backs away.)

Good. Better. Stay right there.

(SALOME enters, carrying what looks like a roast on a tray; the roast is covered with a tea towel.)

SALOME: *(To ALIDA.)* I've brought you your supper. since you're so damned hungry.

ALIDA: Not now, Salome!

SALOME: Yes, now! Are you ready? Are you ready for this?

(SALOME whips the towel from the tray to reveal Mitch's head. Her next lines are delivered through tears but with just a shade of artificiality.)

I didn't think you'd really done it, I thought it was just another lie. How could you really do it?

IAN: My God ...

(ALIDA moves swiftly to SALOME and covers the head with the towel.)

ALIDA: Get out of here with that. Now!

(She shoves SALOME towards the exit.)

SALOME: What am I supposed to do with it?

ALIDA: Bury it. Move!

(SALOME exits.)

IAN: My God.

(ALIDA retrieves the wine, then faces IAN.)

That wasn't real. Was that real?

ALIDA: I think it's time for the truth.

IAN: Oh—boy. I'd better have a look at that. Yeah, definitely. *(Stands, starts off.)*

ALIDA: The truth, Ian.

IAN: Good, great. I'll be right back.

ALIDA: This is a ten second offer.

IAN: *(Stops moving.)* The truth?

ALIDA: *(Brandishes the bottle.)* In vino veritas. Sit down.

IAN: Was that thing real?

ALIDA: Does it matter?

IAN: Does it matter?!

ALIDA: Sit down, Ian.

>*(He obeys.)*

>Are you all right? Going to be sick?

>*(He shakes his head.)*

>You don't feel sorry for him, do you?

IAN: Sorry?

ALIDA: Don't. He's got no one to blame but himself. Now. The truth. What I've orchestrated here tonight is actually a little test.

IAN: A test.

ALIDA: Or you could call it a sort of game, if you wanted to. I've always liked games. Or at any rate, I've always played them.

IAN: What are you talking about?

ALIDA: I need you, Ian. I needed you before but I'm going to need you a lot more now. You can see for yourself what I've done. I've murdered a man. I've murdered the man who was my husband.

IAN: *(Beat.)* No. No, I don't believe that. I don't believe you're capable of that. And even if you were ...

ALIDA: Yes?

IAN: *(Beat.)* I'm supposed to go along with this, right? See where it takes us? I mean, this is—pure speculation.

ALIDA: If you like.

IAN: Okay. So—let's see. You'd, uh—you'd want me to lie for you.

ALIDA: I'd want you to lie with me. *(Smiles.)* I like the sound of that.

IAN: You'd want me to lie to the police.

ALIDA: Oh hell no, I can do that for myself. I need someone to replace Mitch. In my life. I need someone with the same inclination. Someone who doesn't give a damn about other people's rules. Someone who is truly free.

IAN: Free.

ALIDA: Because when you're free, Ian, when you're truly free, you are truly alive. *(Moves in.)* You know what I'm talking about.

IAN: No.

ALIDA: Sure, you do. You know the stuff we do. The stuff you like me doing to you.

IAN: Oh God.

ALIDA: *(Caresses him.)* And, Ian—listen to me. What we've done so far? That was nothing, that was just a taste. It gets better. It gets higher and higher.

IAN: Oh Jesus.

ALIDA: I know what you're thinking. You're thinking you can't push it any higher, but you can. You've got what it takes, I know it. I have some experience in these things and I can tell. I picked you, Ian. Didn't I pick you? Out of thousands. *(Beat.)* Are you all right?

IAN: No, I'm not all right, are you crazy?! I'm mush, for God's sake, I'm—I'm—drowning here.

ALIDA: *(Moves in tighter.)* Poor Ian.

IAN: Don't do that! Stay away from me, do you understand? I'm begging you, Alida. I'm warning you.

(ALIDA kisses him, then suddenly pulls back.)

ALIDA: You beast. You bit me.

IAN: Did I draw blood?

ALIDA: No.

IAN: Well, come here, I'll give it another shot.

ALIDA: *(Beat.)* I need an answer, Ian.

IAN: Tell me you're lying, Alida. You are, aren't you. You didn't really kill him.

ALIDA: Are you going to do it, or not?

IAN: Do ... what exactly?

ALIDA: Whatever we want to do.

IAN: Whatever we—

ALIDA: Whatever we damn well decide we want to do.

IAN: Like this, you mean. Like the sort of thing you've done tonight?

ALIDA: Maybe.

IAN: Like messing around with people's heads.

ALIDA: I don't think I'd put it that way.

IAN: Like murder?

ALIDA: Oh, well. I normally draw the line at that.

IAN: Normally? *(Laughs.)* Good. Good for you, Alida.

(He turns away.)

ALIDA: Look, Ian, it's a very simple thing. Either it appeals to you, or it doesn't. I know it does.

IAN: No.

ALIDA: Yes.

IAN: No!

ALIDA: *(Deadly.)* Then what are you doing here?

IAN: You know what I'm doing here.

ALIDA: I know why you came. Why did you stay?

> *(A beat. They face one another.)*

IAN: Oh no, Jesus, is that what you think? I don't think that's right. I mean, I guess, at a certain level—a certain intellectual level—

ALIDA: I know what you're feeling. You're a little horrified at yourself. Don't be. Ian, listen to me. Nobody gets through life without finding a way to get high. Nobody! Look around you. It's a human condition. I'm just a little more honest about it. And a whole lot more original.

> *(SALOME enters with a garden spade slung across her shoulder.)*

SALOME: Poor Mitch, poor old Mitch.

ALIDA: *(A warning.)* Salome—

SALOME: *(Again, with a trace of artificiality.)* I don't get it, I just don't get it. I don't know why you had to go and kill him. You just … you went out there and—for Pete's sake, you little whore, you chopped his head off. *(Makes a chopping motion.)* Like some old rooster.

ALIDA: *(To SALOME.)* You're going to regret this. You know that, don't you.

SALOME: Oh, shit, that's wrong, isn't it. Let's see. *(Adjusts her manner.)* Well, that's done. But if you think I'm burying the rest of him, you can think again.

ALIDA: I'll bury you in a minute.

SALOME: No, I will not! *(Throws down the spade.)* I've

been cleaning up your messes half my life. No more. Anyway, what's wrong with him? Why can't he do it? Not dressed for it? I'm surprised he's dressed at all, with you in the vicinity.

ALIDA: I warned you, Salome.

SALOME: *(To ALIDA.)* I don't give a shit. I'm sick to death of your lousy stinking second-rate games and I'm sick of playing all the bit parts. I keep telling you I need more scope.

ALIDA: *(Moves to her.)* I'll give you scope.

SALOME: *(Backs off.)* Did you tell him about the scars yet? You better do that. *(To IAN.)* Hey, Ian! Here's a good one for you. I'm the one who gave her her scars.

ALIDA: You did.

SALOME: That's a lie.

ALIDA: *(To IAN.)* She did! I was seven years old. Seven, and she marked me for life. Bitch. Wicked old bitch.

SALOME: Whore. Lying whore.

IAN: *(An explosion.)* Shut up, both of you! My God, you're depraved, I think you're both depraved! Scars, mutilation, murder? *(Laughs crazily.)* What next? When do you stop, what's it going to take to make you stop?!

(A beat. ALIDA turns back to SALOME.)

ALIDA: Get out of here.

SALOME: *(To IAN.)* Have you figured it out yet? Lover?

ALIDA: Get out of here!

SALOME: *(To ALIDA.)* Don't worry, I'm going. Only because I'm ready!

(SALOME exits. ALIDA turns back to IAN.)

IAN: There's no limit to you, is there. There's absolutely nothing you won't say.

ALIDA: She did give me my scars.

IAN: Alida—

ALIDA: She did. Listen, I want you to know this. I used to have fainting spells, when I was a child. Nobody knew what caused them, just—snap, out like a light. And that Salome, that old witch. While I was out, she'd carve me up. With pinking shears! And when anyone would ask—not that anyone often did, not my loving father, certainly—she'd say I'd done it to myself, was always doing it. The minute she turned her back, snip snip snip. Why would a child do a thing like that, didn't anyone ever want to know?

IAN: *(Sits.)* Enough.

ALIDA: Now, of course, she goes in for other forms of entertainment. She seduces young boys—juicy young boys, firm as peaches, who'd rather die horrible deaths than have sex with her. But she forces herself on them. Oh yes. I've seen it. I've been a witness.

   (Silence.)

IAN: *(From a great distance.)* Alida ... you know—know what I'm doing? I'm sitting here—praying—that you're going to walk across to me, and tell me this was all a bad dream, and it's over now, and we can go back to being what we were.

ALIDA: I'm surprised at you. You've been trying for six solid months to find out how I got my scars. Now I tell you, and you act as though you didn't hear.

   (IAN suddenly pulls himself to his feet.)

IAN: I have to get out of here.

ALIDA: Well, I certainly didn't get them in Florence, I can

tell you that. I've never even been there. On the other hand, I have been to Crete. *(Smiles.)*

(IAN casts about in confusion, then begins to gather up his things.)

I take it the answer is no.

(IAN keeps moving.)

You're a fool, you know. Where do you think you're going to go? You can't go back where you came from, they won't have you. You're tainted. You've got an odor about you now, like bad meat. They'll smell you coming a mile away, and bar their doors. They will, the hypocrites. Don't turn your back when I'm talking to you!

IAN: Just let me go, Alida. Okay? While there's still something left of me.

ALIDA: Something left of you! *(Turns away.)* God, what a bore.

IAN: *(Beat.)* Say that again?

ALIDA: You're a bore, a bore, boring. You're smug, self-righteous and narrow-minded, with a mind like pursed lips. Just the sight of you is suffocating to me.

IAN: Well, this is refreshing. What's this, the truth at last?

ALIDA: I tried, I really tried with you, you know that? Hopeless. And now look at you, just look at you! A big—mopey—baby! What are you moping about, anyway? You're not a child. You knew what you were getting into.

IAN: No.

ALIDA: And besides—you'll survive. As a matter of fact, you'll be better for it. As a matter of *fact*, you should thank me. I pulled you out of that cement you were

imbedded in—the cement you called your life—and I
breathed fire into you. You've never been so alive!

IAN: Are you finished?

ALIDA: I'm finished with you.

IAN: That's the best news I've had all night.

> *(He exits.)*

ALIDA: What a waste. *(Moves after him, calls out.)* Ian!
What a waste! Remember I said that.

> *(She stands looking after him for a moment, then
> moves to the lawn chair, sits, stares off. A few
> beats. The window swings open and MITCH steps
> out. He moves quietly in behind her, bends her
> head back, kisses her.)*

MITCH: You'll never guess what I've got. *(Draws a
mickey from his pocket, runs it around her neck.)*
Maybe I'll let you have some, if you're good.

ALIDA: I'm always good.

MITCH: You're never good. That's why I keep you
around.

> *(He kisses her again, then moves to the table to
> pour drinks. She stares off.)*

ALIDA: Look at it, would you? Beautiful. We should get
up here more often, you know that? We should really
make a point of it. *(Glances at him, smiles a secret
smile.)* So. Did it work for you?

MITCH: Sure, why not, you?

ALIDA: You don't sound as though you mean that.

> *(No response. She turns toward him.)*

Mitch?

MITCH: Let's have a drink, Alida.

ALIDA: That's no answer.

MITCH: Let's just have a drink, all right?

> *(MITCH moves back to her, hands her a drink, then moves down right. She drinks, he doesn't. A beat.)*

ALIDA: What's the matter with you?

MITCH: Nothing. I'd like to know where the fuck Salome is.

ALIDA: You surely don't expect her to show up when she's supposed to.

MITCH: Not after your little performance.

ALIDA: My performance! What about hers?

MITCH: You have to coddle her a bit. How many times have I told you that? If you coddle her, she's fine.

ALIDA: *(Stands.)* Well, I'm sick to death of coddling her. She's finished, Mitch. I expect you to back me up on that.

MITCH: *(Deadly.)* You *what*. Expect? Is that what you said?

ALIDA: I—she tried to sabotage me.

MITCH: *(Moves in.)* Who do you think you're talking to, here?

> *(SALOME enters.)*

ALIDA: Okay, Mitch.

MITCH: Save that kind of talk for the bait! *(Turns to SALOME.)* Well?

SALOME: He's gone.

MITCH: Good.

>   *(He turns away.)*

SALOME: I need to talk to you, Mitch.

MITCH: Later.

SALOME: When, later?

MITCH: Tomorrow.

SALOME: Tomorrow? This is important to me.

MITCH: *(Faces her.)* Tomorrow.

SALOME: *(Beat.)* Is that it? That's all you're going to say?

MITCH: Look, Salome—

SALOME: I like to play. I really like to play, you know
that. But I won't take orders from her. I need a free
hand.

ALIDA: Oh, get out of here.

SALOME: *(To ALIDA.)* I'm not talking to you!

MITCH: Okay, both of you—enough.

SALOME: *(To MITCH.)* She kept saying I was drunk. I
wasn't drunk.

ALIDA: You certainly were.

SALOME: I was not!

MITCH: Enough. I'm warning you, Salome—

SALOME: Me? What about her?

ALIDA: She's still drunk, I can smell her from here.

SALOME: Lying whore.

MITCH: *(To SALOME.)* Get the fuck out of here! Now!

>   *(For a moment SALOME doesn't move. Then she
>   starts off.)*

We'll talk tomorrow, Salome. I promise.

(SALOME exits.)

Shit.

ALIDA: You have to coddle her. If you coddle her, she's fine.

MITCH: Sloppy! I'm telling you, this has been one fucking sloppy night.

ALIDA: I wouldn't worry about it.

MITCH: *(Turns on her.)* You wouldn't, eh. Did you get my keys?

ALIDA: Oh hell.

MITCH: Way to go.

ALIDA: I'm sorry, I didn't even think of them.

MITCH: Fuck, Alida, you had your hands all over him.

ALIDA: Well, don't blame me! You're the one who gave them to him.

MITCH: I didn't give them to him, I tossed them to him. You want to know how he caught them? With his tight little ass!

(He moves away. A beat.)

ALIDA: I don't understand what's happening here. You know what I think? Mitch? I think we should back up and start over again. Concentrate on what really matters. *(Glances at him, then moves in behind him.)* What do you think? We can do that, can't we?

MITCH: Not if I have to kiss you again.

(ALIDA starts to move away.)

Hey. *(Grabs her hand; a beat.)* You were dynamite tonight.

ALIDA: Was I?

MITCH: TNT.

ALIDA: You weren't so bad yourself.

>*(They toast one another, drink.)*

Your assessment?

MITCH: *(Shrugs.)* Not bad.

ALIDA: Not bad?

MITCH: Not stupid, not ugly. What do you want?

ALIDA: *(Smiles.)* You're teasing me.

MITCH: Am I?

ALIDA: Come on, Mitch. He was intrigued, he really was.

MITCH: Yeah? Well, he's gone, isn't he.

ALIDA: It was a struggle.

MITCH: It was a struggle, all right. You know why? Because you had that poor bastard dancing on so many strings, he couldn't piss unless you pulled one.

ALIDA: *(Beat.)* What the hell is the matter with you.

MITCH: Look, what do you want? Do you want me to tell you he was good? He was good. You did good.

>*(He salutes her.)*

ALIDA: Do you mean that?

MITCH: Yeah. I thought he was real—nice.

>*(A beat.)*

ALIDA: Nice. What do you mean, nice.

MITCH: It's not a complicated word.

ALIDA: He was not very damn nice and you know it! He *was* nice, once, when I met him—a nice, decent, boring boy. I changed that.

MITCH: I don't think so, Alida.

ALIDA: I did. I set him free, set him on fire, showed him what it means to be alive!

MITCH: You're kidding yourself.

ALIDA: I did! And he proved it, tonight. He was with me every inch of the way. You could see that, you had to see that. Why can't you admit it?

MITCH: Look, you wanted my opinion, you got it.

(*Beat.*)

ALIDA: Well! If that's the way it is, I think I'll have another drink.

MITCH: You don't need another drink.

ALIDA: It's been a long night.

MITCH: About average.

ALIDA: It's been one hell of a long night, and you know it!

MITCH: Hey, don't take it like this. What did you expect me to say, anyway?

ALIDA: I expected you to say he was the best.

MITCH: The best of yours.

ALIDA: The best of the lot.

MITCH: No way. Remember Janice?

ALIDA: No.

MITCH: Sure you do, you remember Janice.

ALIDA: No, I really don't, how could I? One curvaceous little airhead is pretty much like the rest.

MITCH: She was no airhead. She had you on your toes. She made you sweat.

ALIDA: Did she?

MITCH: Don't give me that—did she. You were sizzling. There was steam rising off the lake, and we weren't even in it.

ALIDA: All right!

MITCH: Don't tell me she didn't make you sweat.

ALIDA: But Ian didn't do that. He didn't make you sweat.

MITCH: Sweat, fuck. I could hardly stay awake.

ALIDA: *(Beat.)* That's why you were so rough on him, I guess.

MITCH: I wasn't rough on him.

ALIDA: You certainly were.

MITCH: I wasn't fucking rough! I wanted him out of here, that's all.

ALIDA: Broken whiskey bottles, the works.

MITCH: Well, what can I say? I was panting for my reward.

    (He toasts her, drinks, turns away.)

ALIDA: You're lying to me.

MITCH: Fuck that. Lying.

ALIDA: You are.

MITCH: I almost wish I was, for your sake. I'm not.

ALIDA: Then I'd like to know why you're so fucking mad!

MITCH: *(Beat.)* You jeopardized the game.

ALIDA: What?

MITCH: You jeopardized the whole fucking game, can't you see that?

ALIDA: What are you talking about?

MITCH: You know what I'm talking about.

ALIDA: I haven't the foggiest idea! Now you'd better explain yourself. If you're going to say a thing like that to me, you'd better be able to explain it.

MITCH: No. *(Moves in on her.)* No, you're the one with the explaining to do. You can start right now. You can start by explaining why it took you so fucking long to get him up here. I mean, I know about your appetite. But six months? And then there's all this fiancé stuff he's laying on me. Fiancé this, fiancé that. And the funny thing is, he's serious. He really thinks he's going to do it, he's practically bought the fucking flowers. Now you explain that to me, Alida. I'm really curious about that!

ALIDA: It was because of his background.

MITCH: His what?

ALIDA: His background, he—comes from this very strict background—he was even engaged to some pallid little church-mouse when I met him—and he had to believe it was leading somewhere, that *we* were, or he couldn't—

MITCH: Perform?

ALIDA: He could perform just fine. But he was getting restless, feeling guilty about things, and I had to do something, that's all.

MITCH: You could have dumped him.

ALIDA: What?

MITCH: You heard me. The world is full of men.

ALIDA: *(Beat.)* I didn't want to dump him.

MITCH: You broke the rule, Alida. One rule—very simple, very easy to remember, very important. No complications! You broke it. I want to know why.

ALIDA: I thought you liked a challenge.

MITCH: *(A controlled explosion.)* If you want new rules— if you want a new kind of game—you've got it. I just hope you've got the stomach for it!

> *(He pulls away. A beat.)*

ALIDA: Okay, I broke the rule, I admit it.

MITCH: Why?

ALIDA: My God, isn't it obvious? I thought he could do it. I thought he could really do it—if I groomed him well enough.

MITCH: Do what?

ALIDA: What do you think? For God's sake, there's only one answer to that question.

MITCH: No, Alida. There's two.

> *(She turns toward him. Silence.)*

ALIDA: Is that what this is all about! My God, it is, isn't it. *(Beat.)* I don't know what to say.

MITCH: You'd better think of something. Fast.

ALIDA: So. It's not the game you're upset about—of course not, there's always another game. It's Ian who's upset you. You could see how good he was, a real contender—potentially, a contender—and it scared the hell out of you.

MITCH: I wouldn't go that far.

ALIDA: Come on, Mitch. You've spent the last fifteen

minutes working me over.

MITCH: So?

ALIDA: You were scared to death. Say it.

MITCH: Fuck, Alida—

ALIDA: I need to hear this.

MITCH: Why?

ALIDA: You know why.

MITCH: I'm not sure I do.

ALIDA: Because I want you hot and I want you high. And
I want to know that I did it!

(*MITCH grins.*)

MITCH: Oh, babe. You're something else, you know that?
You can lie your ass off to any man you meet, you can
spin out fantasies that run on for weeks. But when I
want the truth out of you, all I have to do is turn the key.
Why is that? Huh? Get over here.

ALIDA: Not until you say it.

MITCH: All right, I was scared. I was fucking scared, all
right? For maybe three seconds.

ALIDA: You thought I really wanted him.

MITCH: It crossed my mind.

ALIDA: I can't believe it. This is wonderful.

MITCH: Yeah well, don't gloat too much, Alida. You had
to change the game, to do it. That's what threw me, if
you want to know. I mean, it's one thing to come up
here and have to watch some pimply-faced kid who's
been screwing your ass off prance around like he's the
only one who knows how to do it—that's one thing.
This fiancé stuff—this six months business—that's

something else.

ALIDA: *(Beat.)* You're the only one I've ever loved. You know that.

MITCH: Are you going to get over here, or what.

ALIDA: *(Moves to him.)* I don't blame you for being scared, though. He was quite a specimen. And you know what? Mitch? He was very good.

MITCH: Don't give me that.

ALIDA: *(Caresses him.)* He was.

MITCH: How good?

ALIDA: As good as I've ever had.

MITCH: Liar. *(Grabs her hair, pulls her head back.)* Liar.

ALIDA: Pants on fire.

MITCH: I'm going to show you what I do to liars.

> *(He kisses her, undoes her robe, moves in tight. Hot stuff. IAN enters, with a rifle. He is very wired. He moves silently in behind MITCH and puts the nose of the rifle against MITCH's neck. MITCH freezes. Then ALIDA freezes.)*

IAN: Don't stop on my account. I said don't stop!

> *(MITCH tries to turn.)*

Don't turn.

> *(MITCH freezes again.)*

It's your rifle and it's loaded. You know it's loaded. Now go ahead—fuck her. Come on, that's what this is all about, right?

MITCH: No.

IAN: *(Jabs him with the rifle.)* Yes! I've been out there,

listening. I've had an earful! Now you fuck her, damn you.

MITCH: You're making a mistake.

IAN: Shut up and fuck her!

MITCH: *(Beat.)* Come here, Alida. Come here!

> *(ALIDA moves into MITCH's arms. He kisses her woodenly.)*

IAN: That's right, do it. Come on, do it. Do it! You call that doing it?

MITCH: You son of a bitch—

IAN: *(Jams the rifle into his neck.)* I want to see a little steam here. I want to see steam rising off the lake, you know? I paid for it, God damn it. I sold myself for this. You think that's fun? Man? *(Jabs MITCH with the rifle.)* Think that's a picnic? *(Jabs him again.)* Now you show me some action. Man! Show me how good I was!

ALIDA: Ian, for God's sake—

IAN: *(Swings the rifle on her.)* You are not talking! Understand?

MITCH: *(Pulls her into him.)* She understands.

IAN: She better!

MITCH: She does.

IAN: Good. *(To MITCH.)* Now take your clothes off. Take your clothes off so you can do it!

> *(MITCH takes off his jacket.)*

That's it. Now your shirt. Your shirt!

> *(MITCH starts to unbutton his shirt.)*

Good. Very good. You're pretty smart, for a dead man.

(To ALIDA.) What are you looking like that for?
You're not scared, are you? I thought you liked this
sort of thing. Or maybe you only like it when you get
to call the shots. Stop looking like that! I'm not going
to shoot you. *(Laughs crazily.)* Not until you finish,
anyway.

> *(MITCH takes off his shirt.)*

(To MITCH.) Good. Hey, this is pretty good. Now keep
going. Keep going!

> *(MITCH pulls one running shoe off, then the other.
> Then he starts on his pants.)*

Oh yeah, this is going to work. It's going to work out
fine. You're going to like this, both of you. It's going
to give you a whole new perspective on—on what?
Humiliation! Oh, yeah. I think so.

> *(SALOME enters.)*

SALOME: What's going on here?

> *(IAN swings so that he can keep a line on all three
> of them.)*

IAN: Don't move! Don't anybody move!

SALOME: *(To IAN.)* What the hell do you think you're
doing?

IAN: Get out of here, Salome!

SALOME: Put that thing down.

IAN: Get out of here or I'll blow you away!

SALOME: You might.

> *(SALOME takes a step towards IAN. He swings to
> face her. As he does, MITCH suddenly lunges at
> IAN. IAN turns and fires. MITCH crumples.
> There's a moment of stunned disbelief; no one*

moves. Then ALIDA drops to her knees next to MITCH.)

ALIDA: Mitch?

(SALOME runs to MITCH, kneels beside him.)

IAN: Oh my God. Oh my God ...

ALIDA: Mitch! Answer me.

(For a moment, both women try to rouse MITCH; no luck. Suddenly ALIDA shakes him violently.)

Answer me!

(SALOME starts to cry.)

SALOME: Oh no. Oh no, Mitch.

ALIDA: He's dead.

(IAN is profoundly shocked by what he has done. His chest starts to heave. He turns on ALIDA.)

IAN: Is this the idea? Hey—hey, Alida! Think I've got the hang of it now? Look at me, God damn you, I want an answer! Is this the kind of high you're after?!

(No response. IAN tries to get himself in hand, can't do it. He becomes aware of the rifle in his hands and throws it down in disgust. He backs away, stares around in confusion, then starts to stumble off. As he does, ALIDA slowly reaches for the rifle, picks it up and gets to her feet.)

ALIDA: Ian? Sweetheart?

(She raises the rifle and trains it on him. He stops moving, turns to face her. Blackout. The end.)

MORE CANADIAN DRAMA TITLES AVAILABLE FROM BLIZZARD PUBLISHING

Bordertown Café

by Kelly Rebar
104 pp. 51/2 x 8 1/2 in.
0-921368-08-9 $9.95 (pb)

The Mail Order Bride

by Robert Clinton
Winner of the 1988 Alberta Playwrighting Competition.
96 pp. 51/2 x 8 1/2 in.
0-921368-09-7 $8.95 (pb)

Footprints On The Moon

by Maureen Hunter
Nominated for the 1988 Governor General's Award.
96 pp. 5 1/2 x 8 1/2 in.
0-921368-07-0 $8.95 (pb)

Sky

by Connie Gault
80 pp. 5 1/2 x 8 1/2 in.
0-921368-06-2 $8.95 (pb)

The Chinese Man Said Goodbye

by Bruce McManus
80 pp. 5 1/2 x 8 1/2 in.
0-921368-05-4 $8.95 (pb)

The Third Ascent

by Frank Moher
Winner of the 1988 Sterling Award for Outstanding New Play.
80 pp. 5 1/2 x 8 1/2 in.
0-921368-04-6 $8.95 (pb)

refugees

by Harry Rintoul
96 pp. 5 x 8 in.
0-921368-02-X $7.95 (pb)